BUILT DIFFERENT

A Daily Devotional for Business Leaders

DAVID ANGERON

TABLE OF CONTENTS

INTRODUCTION

Built Different: A 365-Day Devotional for Business Leaders
The business world isn't for the faint of heart. It demands long hours, bold decisions, high pressure, thick skin, and a mindset willing to carry responsibility when others crumble under it. But leadership was never meant to be powered by human strength alone.

There is a remnant of business leaders who refuse to separate faith from their work — leaders who believe the boardroom is a mission field, that success is stewardship, and that influence is responsibility. These leaders don't just build companies — they build people, culture, integrity, and legacy.

They are built different.

If you picked up this devotional, it's because something inside you knows there is more to leadership than revenue goals and quarterly metrics. Deep down, you know your calling in business is spiritual. You know the decisions you make affect lives, families, and futures. You know influence is a gift God expects you to steward well.

You are not just in business — you are in ministry with a different assignment.

This devotional was written to strengthen the leader behind the leadership — the inner world that fuels the external world. Every day of this year, you will be:

- ♦ Encouraged spiritually
- ♦ Challenged mentally
- ♦ Sharpened as a leader
- ♦ Grounded in Scripture
- ♦ Strengthened in identity, character, and purpose

You'll be reminded that:
- ♦ Excellence is worship.
- ♦ Strategy is stewardship.
- ♦ Growth is obedience.

1

- ♦ Influence is responsibility.
- ♦ Leadership is discipleship.

And through every season — busy, blessed, pressured, or painful — God will shape you into the leader He designed you to be, not the leader the world pressures you to become.

This devotional is not about becoming *famous* — it's about becoming *faithful.*

Not about becoming *successful* — but *significant.*

Not about gaining *position* — but embracing *purpose.*

Leadership gets heavy — but you were not called to carry it alone.

As you walk through these 365 days, my prayer is that you will:

- ♦ Lead boldly
- ♦ Love deeply
- ♦ Work excellently
- ♦ Think strategically
- ♦ Live gratefully
- ♦ And finish faithfully

Because when a leader is spiritually strong, the business becomes a ministry, the workplace becomes a mission field, and every decision becomes an opportunity to glorify God.

You are a business leader on purpose, for purpose, and with purpose.

You are Built Different.

Let's grow — one day at a time.

— *Coach David Angeron*

ACKNOWLEDGMENTS

Projects like this are never accomplished alone. Though the words on these pages came through my pen, the strength behind them came from the people God placed in my life.

To my **Lord and Savior Jesus Christ** — thank You for the calling, the assignment, the wisdom, and the grace that makes leadership possible. Every insight, every lesson, and every breakthrough in this devotional belongs to You.

To my **wife, my best friend, my partner in purpose** — thank you for your unwavering support, your encouragement during long nights of writing, and your belief in every dream God has given us. Your love and strength make the impossible possible.

To my **children and family** — you are my legacy and my motivation. I pray this devotional not only blesses others but becomes a spiritual blueprint for you as you pursue your God-given purpose.

To the **mentors, pastors, coaches, leaders, and friends** who have invested in my life — thank you for the wisdom, accountability, and truth you have spoken into me over the years. Leadership is sharpened by iron, and my life has been shaped by the iron God surrounded me with.

To the **business leaders, entrepreneurs, and executives around the world** who carry the weight of responsibility with excellence and faith — you inspire this mission. You are proof that leadership and faith do not compete, but complete one another.

To every **reader who picked up this devotional** — thank you for allowing me to speak into your life for the next 365 days. My prayer is that each page brings strength to your soul, clarity to your calling, and courage to your leadership.

And to everyone who has supported this journey in ways seen and unseen — prayers, encouragement, partnership, and belief in the vision — thank you. You are part of this story.

May the words of this devotional strengthen leaders for generations.

May it point every reader to Christ, the source of all wisdom, excellence, and purpose.

— *Coach David Angeron*

JANUARY

FOUNDATIONS OF A FAITH-DRIVEN LEADER

January 1 — Built to Influence

Y ou weren't called into business simply to make income — you were called to make impact. The marketplace is one of the greatest mission fields on the planet, and every leader who follows Christ carries influence in places pastors may never step foot. God didn't place you in the business world by accident. You are positioned, on purpose, for purpose.

Leadership isn't just what you do — it's who you become in front of others. People are watching how you solve problems, how you treat others, how you respond under pressure, and how you speak when no one can benefit you. Influence is not built in moments of reward, but in moments of responsibility.

When your decisions reflect Christ, people notice. When your excellence is consistent, people trust you. When your character remains stable, people follow you. God elevates leaders not so others can applaud them, but so others can find Him through them.

You don't need a microphone to lead. You don't need a title to influence. You just need to show up every day with integrity, humility, and excellence — the world is already watching.

Reflection Questions

1. Where has God intentionally placed me to influence people in this season?

2. What habits or attitudes do I need to strengthen so my leadership reflects Christ more consistently?

Author Quote — Coach David Angeron

"You don't influence people by telling them who you are — you influence them by proving it every day when no one is keeping score."

January 2 —
Excellence Is Evangelism

"Whatever you do, work at it with all your heart, as working for the Lord, not for men." — Colossians 3:23

In the business world, excellence is one of the loudest forms of evangelism. People may not agree with your beliefs, but they cannot ignore your results. A Christian leader shouldn't just *talk* differently — they should *work* differently. Excellence earns respect, influence, and opportunity.

Excellence doesn't require perfection — it requires intention. It means doing your very best even when no one would know if you cut corners. It means showing up prepared, finishing what you start, and taking pride in the details that others overlook. People trust leaders who take their work seriously.

When you operate with excellence, you represent God well. Excellence attracts opportunity. Excellence builds credibility. Excellence earns a voice. And when God gives you a voice, He expects you to use it boldly and humbly.

Your work is more than a paycheck — it's worship. Honor God today with excellence, and let the results speak for you.

Reflection Questions

1. In what area of my work have I allowed "good enough" to replace excellence?

2. What small changes can I make today to honor God through higher standards?

Author Quote — Coach David Angeron

"Excellence doesn't require more resources — it requires more responsibility for what you already have."

January 3 —
Purpose Before Promotions

Promotion is a blessing, but purpose is the assignment. Many leaders chase titles, raises, and recognition — yet overlook the greatest reward: living the purpose God designed. A promotion can elevate you; purpose can transform you.

When you chase purpose, promotions follow as a byproduct. When you chase promotions, purpose often gets lost in the process. God elevates leaders who are more committed to His mission than to their own status. True influence isn't achieved when you arrive at the top — it begins when you choose obedience over ambition.

Instead of asking, *"How do I get ahead?"*, ask, *"How do I grow what God has placed in my hands today?"* Purpose requires patience, humility, and surrender. But when you align your work with God's will, your steps become ordered, and your influence multiplies.

Let your purpose lead — and your promotions will never define you.

Reflection Questions

1. Am I driven more by purpose or by personal advancement?
2. How can I honor God within the position I currently have?

Author Quote — Coach David Angeron

"If you chase purpose, promotions become inevitable — but if you chase promotions, purpose becomes invisible."

January 4 —
Values Over Velocity

"The integrity of the upright guides them." — Proverbs 11:3

The pace of business can make you feel like you need to prove something — to yourself, to others, or to the world. But speed without values is self-destruction disguised as progress. Leadership without a moral compass leads companies into culture drift, chaos, and compromise.

Slow success built on values is better than fast success built on shortcuts. You never win long-term by sacrificing integrity for opportunity. A leader who refuses to compromise becomes someone God can trust with greater influence.

Your calendar may be full, your goals may be aggressive, and your expectations may be high — but none of that should outrun your character. Values must determine your velocity.

Move fast, but never faster than your integrity.

Reflection Questions

1. Where am I tempted to sacrifice values for speed or convenience?
2. Which personal standard needs reinforcement this week?

Author Quote — Coach David Angeron

"If success costs you your convictions, then the price is too high no matter the reward."

JANUARY 5 — LEADING WITHOUT LOSING YOURSELF

"What good will it be for someone to gain the whole world, yet forfeit their soul?" — Matthew 16:26

Too many leaders win at work but lose at life. They build empires while watching their foundation crack. They create success while quietly unraveling. It is possible to lead with excellence externally while collapsing internally.

Leadership does not require losing yourself. God never called you to sacrifice mental health, joy, marriage, faith, or family for the sake of success. The enemy would love to keep you so busy winning in the marketplace that you forget who you are in the Kingdom.

There will always be another deadline, another goal, another opportunity. But there will never be another you. The best gift you can give your business, your team, and your family is a healthy, grounded, spiritually strong leader.

Lead boldly — but never abandon yourself in the process.

Reflection Questions

1. Where do I feel myself stretching too thin emotionally, mentally, or spiritually?

2. What boundaries would help me stay whole while I lead?

Author Quote — Coach David Angeron

"Leadership is not about losing yourself to win — it's about becoming who God created you to be while you win."

January 6 —
Pressure Reveals Calling

"Consider it pure joy, my brothers and sisters, whenever you face trials of many kinds." — James 1:2

Pressure exposes what comfort hides. Anyone can feel called when leadership is easy — but true calling is proven when stress hits, when responsibility increases, and when weight gets heavy. Pressure doesn't weaken a leader; it *reveals* one.

If the assignment on your life feels heavy, it's because God trusted you to carry something significant. Pressure is not punishment — it's preparation. It builds spiritual muscle, emotional toughness, and mental resilience. God trains leaders by stretching them.

Don't pray the pressure away — pray for the strength to grow through it. Many leaders ask God to remove weight that He is using to increase capacity. Pressure is not proof that you're failing — it's proof that you're called.

If you weren't built for this, you wouldn't be facing it.

Reflection Questions

1. What pressure am I currently facing that may be preparing me rather than defeating me?

2. How can I rely on God for strength instead of asking for escape?

Author Quote — Coach David Angeron

"Pressure doesn't prove you're overwhelmed — it proves God trusts you with something worth carrying."

January 7 —
Identity Before Industry

The world identifies you by what you *do*. God identifies you by who you *are*. Business titles change. Roles evolve. Opportunities shift. But your identity in Christ is unshakable.

If your identity is rooted in performance, success will make you prideful and failure will make you worthless. But if your identity is rooted in Christ, success becomes a platform and failure becomes a teacher — neither defines you.

Before you are a CEO, manager, entrepreneur, or leader — you are a child of God. You lead *from* identity, not *for* identity. You don't have to prove yourself worthy — you already are.

When you remember who you are, you'll never lose yourself in what you do.

Reflection Questions

1. Where have I been defining myself by performance rather than identity in Christ?

2. How would my leadership decisions change if I led from confidence instead of insecurity?

Author Quote — Coach David Angeron

"When you know who you are in Christ, you no longer need titles, trophies, or applause to feel valuable."

January 8 —
The Standard You Set, You Become

"But as for me and my household, we will serve the Lord."
— Joshua 24:15

Your life follows the standards you set, not the goals you announce. Goals motivate — but standards transform. Standards determine behaviors, habits, and culture. A company becomes whatever its leader tolerates.

If you want stronger discipline, raise your standard. If you want better results, raise your standard. If you want a culture of excellence, raise your personal standard first. Leaders don't rise to the level of their intentions — they rise to the level of their standards.

You teach people how to treat you by what you accept. You teach people how to perform by what you reward. You teach people what matters by what you repeat. Everything rises and falls with standards.

Set a higher one today.

Reflection Questions

1. Which personal or team standards have slipped and need reinforcement?

2. How would raising my standard in one area affect everything else?

Author Quote — Coach David Angeron

*"Your standards shape your future more
than your goals ever will."*

January 9 — Consistency Is a Leadership Superpower

Consistency is the difference between leaders who talk about excellence and leaders who achieve it. Anyone can be disciplined for a day — champions are disciplined for seasons. Long-term results aren't built through motivation — they're built through consistency.

Consistency does not mean perfection. It means showing up when you don't feel inspired. It means finishing what you start. It means doing the right things repeatedly until the results manifest.

Your team will not follow someone who performs unpredictably. Stability breeds trust. Trust breeds influence. Influence breeds impact.

Keep showing up. Even when it feels slow. Even when no one notices. Even when results seem delayed. Consistency always pays.

Reflection Questions

1. In what area of leadership have I been inconsistent?
2. What small, repeatable habit can I commit to this week?

Author Quote — Coach David Angeron

"Consistency is the bridge between intention and transformation."

January 10 — Growth Begins Where Comfort Ends

Comfort is the silent killer of leadership. Nothing extraordinary grows in a comfort zone. If you're too comfortable, you're not growing — and if you're growing, you're not comfortable. God stretches leaders to prepare them for greater assignments.

Growth requires risk, vulnerability, discomfort, and exposure. It requires stepping into situations where outcomes aren't guaranteed. The enemy wants you safe; God wants you stretched.

Don't confuse discomfort with danger — sometimes discomfort is evidence that God is expanding you. The places that feel the most unfamiliar often hold the greatest breakthroughs.

Lean into the stretch. Growth waits there.

Reflection Questions

1. What comfort zone do I need to exit to obey God's calling in this season?

2. What opportunity have I been delaying because it feels unfamiliar or risky?

Author Quote — Coach David Angeron

"Comfort creates leaders who survive — discomfort creates leaders who grow."

January 11 — When God Opens a Door, Walk Through It

Some opportunities are optional — others are ordained. There will be moments in your leadership journey when God makes it undeniably clear: *This is your door.* It may not look convenient or comfortable, but it will be aligned with your calling.

Open doors don't always look impressive at first glance. They often start small, require humility, or feel beyond your current capacity. That's because God opens doors not for who you are now, but for who you're becoming.

When God opens a door, no competitor, critic, or circumstance can close it. You don't have to force what God has favored. Your responsibility is to walk through in faith — not wait in fear.

If He opened it, you're ready.

Reflection Questions

1. What opportunity have I been hesitant to walk into, even though I sense God opened it?

2. Am I delaying obedience because I'm waiting to feel more prepared?

Author Quote — Coach David Angeron

"God doesn't open doors based on where you are — He opens them based on where He's taking you."

January 12 —
Stewardship Over Ownership

"Now it is required that those who have been given a trust must prove faithful." — 1 Corinthians 4:2

Leadership is not ownership — it's stewardship. Everything you lead, build, influence, or manage ultimately belongs to God. The business, the resources, the talent around you, and the opportunities before you — all of it is entrusted to you for a season.

Owners protect *their* interests. Stewards protect *God's* interests. When you view leadership through stewardship, decisions become clearer. Pride decreases. Humility increases. And pressure shifts from *self-made* to *God-trusted*.

God multiplies what is stewarded well. He promotes leaders not because they demand more, but because they have proven faithful with what they already have. The fastest path to more is faithfulness with the little.

Lead like a steward — and God will treat you like a partner.

Reflection Questions

1. Where have I been acting like an owner instead of a steward?

2. What resource, relationship, or responsibility is God trusting me to manage better?

Author Quote — Coach David Angeron

"God never promised to fund your ego — but He will always fund His purpose through faithful stewards."

January 13 — Competitive Greatness With Kingdom Character

There is nothing unspiritual about being competitive. God did not call leaders to be passive, timid, or indifferent — He called them to dominate their assignment with skill, grit, and excellence. The problem isn't competitiveness — it's competitiveness without character.

Competitive greatness means you strive to be the best *while honoring God in how you get there.* You don't manipulate deals, tear people down, play dirty, or compromise your values for the win. Winning without integrity is just losing in disguise.

Be fierce — but be fair. Fight hard — but fight clean. Build big — but build with character. Your work ethic may impress people, but your character will impact them.

Greatness without integrity is temporary. Greatness with integrity is legacy.

Reflection Questions

1. Where in my ambition do I need to reinforce character?

2. What does "winning the right way" look like in my industry?

Author Quote — Coach David Angeron

"Real greatness isn't just about beating the competition — it's about honoring God while you win."

January 14 —
Leaders Are Built in the Dark

"He will strengthen you and help you." — Isaiah 41:10

Public leadership is produced in private battles. The moments of obscurity — the unseen sacrifices, early mornings, late nights, doubts you never shared, and prayers you whispered through exhaustion — that's where God forms leaders.

Most people only notice the results — not the refining. They notice the platform — not the process. Promotion comes suddenly, but preparation comes slowly. God builds leaders long before He displays them.

When it feels like no one sees your effort, God does. When it feels like no one understands your calling, God does. When it feels like no one appreciates the weight you carry, God does. You are not being overlooked — you are being developed.

Your private faithfulness is shaping your public future.

Reflection Questions

1. What part of my preparation season have I been resenting instead of embracing?

2. Where is God strengthening me behind the scenes right now?

Author Quote — Coach David Angeron

"Before God promotes leaders publicly, He prepares them privately."

January 15 —
Integrity Is Non-Negotiable

Integrity is the backbone of leadership. When a leader's integrity collapses, the organization eventually follows. Skills attract opportunities — but integrity sustains them.

Talent may get you in the room, results may get you noticed, and influence may increase your platform — but only integrity will allow you to stay. Without integrity, success has an expiration date.

Integrity means telling the truth when lying is easier. Doing the right thing when the wrong thing is more profitable. Honoring commitments when breaking them would be more convenient. It costs something — but the reward is immeasurable.

A leader may impress the world with accomplishments, but they impact the world with integrity.

Reflection Questions

1. Is there an area where I need to choose integrity over convenience or profit?

2. What personal boundary protects my character when no one is watching?

Author Quote — Coach David Angeron

"Integrity isn't what you stand for when watched — it's what you refuse to compromise when no one sees."

January 16 —
Honor Up, Down, and Around

Honor is not about position — it's about posture. Some leaders only show honor upward — to those who can give them opportunity. Others show honor downward — to those who follow them. But leaders who are **built different** honor *everyone*.

Honor upward → respecting authority.

Honor downward → protecting and valuing those you lead.

Honor around → supporting peers without jealousy or rivalry.

Honor builds unity. Dishonor breeds division. You cannot build a healthy culture on dishonor. Honor must be the *culture*, not just a "value" on the wall.

Honor the people above you. Honor the people beside you. Honor the people below you. Respect will come back multiplied.

Reflection Questions

1. Who in my life or organization needs more honor from me?

2. Where do I need to remove complaining, sarcasm, or criticism from my leadership posture?

Author Quote — Coach David Angeron

"Honor doesn't flow just one direction — real leaders honor up, down, and around."

January 17 —
Choosing Mission People

"Do not be misled: Bad company corrupts good character."
— 1 Corinthians 15:33

You can't fulfill a God-sized mission with small-minded people. The people around you are either fueling your calling or fighting it. You don't need perfect people — but you need *mission people.*

Mission people:
♦ Push you toward purpose
♦ Celebrate your growth
♦ Protect your blind spots
♦ Pray for you, not preying on you
♦ Add value instead of draining energy

Not everyone can go where God is taking you. Some people belong to your history — not your destiny. Distance doesn't mean hate; it means maturity. Letting go of the wrong relationships makes room for the right ones.

Surround yourself with people who sharpen your faith, accelerate your leadership, and challenge you to become the best version of yourself.

Reflection Questions

1. Who in my circle pushes me toward God's purpose — and who pulls me away from it?

2. What boundaries or shifts do I need to make in my relationships?

Author Quote — Coach David Angeron

"Your future is shaped more by who walks with you than by what stands against you."

January 18 —
Success Requires Sacrifice

"To whom much is given, much will be required." — Luke 12:48

Success is expensive — and the price is paid in sacrifice. You cannot build something great and live like everyone else. Leaders who want exceptional results must embrace exceptional discipline.

Sacrifice may look like:

- ◆ Waking up earlier
- ◆ Eliminating distractions
- ◆ Choosing accountability
- ◆ Saying no to instant gratification
- ◆ Investing time in mastery

God calls leaders to a lifestyle that others may not understand. Not because He wants to punish you — but because He wants to prepare you. Sacrifice becomes the separating line between the average and the anointed.

If you're not willing to sacrifice for your calling, your calling will eventually become a sacrifice.

Reflection Questions

1. What sacrifice is God asking me to make in this season?

2. Where have I been choosing comfort over calling?

Author Quote — Coach David Angeron

"If you want what others don't have, you must commit to what others won't do."

January 19 — The Pace of Purpose

L eaders get in trouble when they try to outrun God — or when they refuse to move when He says go. Purpose has a pace, and wisdom is discerning what season you're in.

There will be seasons of:

- ♦ Building
- ♦ Planting
- ♦ Waiting
- ♦ Accelerating
- ♦ Pruning
- ♦ Harvest

If you rush a planting season, you'll sabotage growth. If you sleep during a harvest season, opportunities will pass by. Your frustration may not be about *where* you are — but about *when* you are.

Purpose has timing. God uses seasons to develop you, protect you, and position you.

Don't force the pace. Follow it.

Reflection Questions

1. What season am I currently in — planting, building, pruning, or harvesting?

2. Have I been resisting God's pace by moving too fast or too slow?

Author Quote — Coach David Angeron

"Purpose has a pace — and peace comes from matching God's timing, not forcing your own."

January 20 — When Opposition Confirms Assignment

"No weapon forged against you will prevail." — Isaiah 54:17

The enemy does not attack what he is not afraid of. Opposition is not always a sign that you're doing something wrong — sometimes it is evidence that you're doing exactly what God called you to do.

When you step into your assignment:

♦ Resistance increases

♦ Critics appear

♦ Doubt whispers

♦ Distractions multiply

Why? Because influence threatens darkness. The enemy wants you discouraged, isolated, and second-guessing your calling. But what comes against you cannot cancel what God placed inside you.

Opposition doesn't mean stop — it means strengthen. If the attack is increasing, so is your assignment.

Stand firm. Your calling is bigger than your conflict.

Reflection Questions

1. Where have I mistaken spiritual opposition for failure or weakness?

2. How can I reinforce my faith instead of retreating in fear?

Author Quote — Coach David Angeron

"Attack is often confirmation —
the enemy fights hardest where God is moving strongest."

January 21 — Faith Over Fear in Decision-Making

Leadership requires decisions — and decisions require courage. Fear will always attempt to negotiate with your faith. Every major decision has two voices attached: one from God and one from fear. One calls you forward; the other calls you to stay safe.

Fear exaggerates risk and minimizes reward. Fear imagines failure but never imagines favor. Faith doesn't remove uncertainty — it removes *limitation.* Leaders who make decisions based on fear build small futures; leaders who make decisions based on faith build the future God intended.

God didn't give you a spirit of fear — so don't borrow one from others. Pray, discern, seek counsel, and then move boldly. Fear is loud, but faith is louder if you choose to listen.

Reflection Questions

1. What decision am I delaying because of fear rather than wisdom?

2. What would I do differently if I fully trusted that God was with me?

Author Quote — Coach David Angeron

"Fear sees danger — faith sees destiny."

January 22 — Gratitude Makes Leaders Magnetic

"Give thanks in all circumstances." — 1 Thessalonians 5:18

Nothing increases influence faster than gratitude. Teams don't flourish under entitlement — they flourish under appreciation. Gratitude builds trust, boosts morale, and unlocks loyalty.

Leaders who are grateful:

- Notice people
- Celebrate progress
- Encourage effort
- Honor contribution

Gratitude doesn't ignore problems — it simply refuses to let problems overshadow blessings. When a leader is thankful, others enjoy working with them. When a leader is never satisfied, people begin looking for a way out.

Gratitude is not just a feeling — it is a practice. The more you express it, the more your influence grows.

Reflection Questions

1. Who on my team deserves specific appreciation today?
2. How can I turn gratitude into a leadership habit instead of an occasional reaction?

Author Quote — Coach David Angeron

"A grateful leader doesn't just get results — they inspire people to help create them."

January 23 —
Excellence Without Arrogance

Some people assume humility means thinking less of yourself. It doesn't. Humility means thinking of yourself *less*. You can be excellent without becoming arrogant. You can be confident without becoming prideful.

Humility does not diminish excellence — it purifies it. Excellence with ego builds empires. Excellence with humility builds people. One demands followers; the other develops leaders.

The more God elevates you, the lower you should bow. Success should never shrink humility — it should strengthen it. When humility and excellence walk together, God can trust you with influence that lasts.

Reflection Questions

1. When I succeed, do I make it about me — or about the mission, the team, and God?

2. Where can I elevate humility in how I communicate and lead?

Author Quote — Coach David Angeron

"Excellence gets you noticed — humility keeps you respected."

January 24 — Mental Toughness for the Marketplace

"For as he thinks in his heart, so is he." — Proverbs 23:7

Business leadership is mentally demanding. The pressure to perform, compete, innovate, and stay ahead can create exhaustion and doubt if your mindset isn't strong. Mental toughness doesn't mean avoiding emotion — it means not surrendering to negative emotion.

Your mind determines your momentum. If your thoughts are discouraged, distracted, fearful, or defeated, performance follows. Leadership demands resilience, focus, and emotional stability — not perfection, but perseverance.

Guard your thoughts fiercely:

- ◆ Filter negativity
- ◆ Reject insecurity
- ◆ Speak Scripture
- ◆ Focus on progress
- ◆ Refuse self-pity

If the enemy can break your mind, he doesn't need to break your business — everything else will fall on its own.

Reflection Questions

1. What thoughts are weakening my confidence and diluting my calling?

2. What Biblical truth do I need to declare over my mindset daily?

Author Quote — Coach David Angeron

"A leader's greatest battlefield is between their ears —
win there, and you win everywhere."

January 25 —
The Price of High Standards

"To whom much is given, much will be required." — Luke 12:48

High standards come with a cost. They require discipline, sacrifice, consistency, and accountability. Not everyone will understand. Some will criticize. Some will leave. But high standards attract high performers.

When God calls you to lead, He calls you to be uncommon. If you lower your standards to make people comfortable, you will create the very culture you fear. Weak standards produce weak results — and weak leaders.

Standards define identity. They set the tone, raise expectations, and protect culture. If you stand firm, the right people will rise to meet your standard.

Greatness demands standards — and standards demand strength.

Reflection Questions

1. Where have I lowered a standard to avoid conflict or discomfort?

2. What expectation do I need to reinforce immediately?

Author Quote — Coach David Angeron

"If your standards don't stretch people, they won't shape people."

January 26 — Leading With Empathy

"Carry each other's burdens." — Galatians 6:2

Empathy is not weakness — it is wisdom. It doesn't remove accountability; it strengthens it. When people feel understood, they become more coachable, loyal, and motivated.

Leaders who lack empathy demand performance but destroy morale. Leaders with empathy elevate people while still requiring greatness. The most successful cultures blend **high expectations** with **high care**.

You never lose influence by caring — you lose influence by ignoring the needs of the people you lead. Empathy earns hearts, and hearts build companies.

Reflection Questions

1. Where have I been too focused on results and not focused enough on people?

2. Who on my team needs support, encouragement, or attention this week?

Author Quote — Coach David Angeron

"Accountability builds performance — empathy builds people."

January 27 — Spiritual Strength for Corporate Stress

"My grace is sufficient for you, for My power is made perfect in weakness."
— 2 Corinthians 12:9

The more responsibility you carry, the more spiritual strength you will need. Stress is not proof you're in the wrong place — sometimes it's proof that you're carrying weight others cannot.

Trying to lead from your own strength leads to burnout, anxiety, and emotional collapse. But leading from God's strength creates resilience, clarity, peace, and endurance.

You weren't designed to carry everything alone. Allow God to strengthen you daily — not occasionally. The demands of leadership are constant; your connection to God must be constant too.

Reflection Questions

1. Where am I trying to lead from my own strength instead of God's strength?

2. What daily spiritual habit do I need to prioritize to stay strong?

Author Quote — Coach David Angeron

"Stress drains leaders — God sustains leaders."

JANUARY 28 —
THE POWER OF QUIET CONFIDENCE

"In quietness and trust is your strength." — Isaiah 30:15

The most powerful leaders don't need to announce their strength — they carry it quietly. Quiet confidence is not silence; it is stability. It is the calm assurance that God is with you, guiding you, backing you, and preparing the way.

Insecurity shouts. Ego brags. Pride postures. But confidence — real confidence — is steady, collected, and secure. It doesn't need to compare, compete, or perform for approval.

The world honors loud confidence. God honors quiet confidence.

Let your confidence come not from titles or accomplishments, but from identity and calling.

Reflection Questions

1. Do I operate more from insecurity or quiet confidence?

2. How can I show strength without needing to prove anything?

Author Quote — Coach David Angeron

"True confidence isn't loud — it's unshakeable."

January 29 —
A Leader Worth Following

"Follow me as I follow Christ." — 1 Corinthians 11:1

Leadership isn't about authority — it's about example. A title can make people listen, but character makes people follow. The greatest leaders are not those who demand respect, but those who **earn** it.

A leader worth following:

- ♦ Lives what they teach
- ♦ Owns their mistakes
- ♦ Works harder than they require
- ♦ Gives credit freely
- ♦ Protects their people
- ♦ Serves more than they command

Leadership is not about being on top — it's about lifting others up. Your greatest credibility comes not from what you *say*, but from how you *live*.

Reflection Questions

1. Would I want to work for a leader who leads the way I do?
2. What area of my example needs strengthening?

Author Quote — Coach David Angeron

"You cannot lead people where you are unwilling to go yourself."

January 30 — God Over Goals

Goals matter — but God matters more. Strategy is essential — but surrender is powerful. Dreams are important — but obedience is everything. Sometimes God will ask you to release a plan you love to receive a purpose you were born for.

Goals without God lead to achievement without fulfillment. But goals *with* God lead to impact, joy, purpose, and legacy. When your goals align with God's will, work becomes worship and success becomes significance.

Plan boldly. Build aggressively. Work diligently. But keep your heart surrendered. Let God interrupt, redirect, revise, and expand your goals at any time — His version is always bigger.

Reflection Questions

1. Are my goals helping me fulfill God's purpose, or competing with it?

2. Where do I need to surrender plans and give God full authority?

Author Quote — Coach David Angeron

"Let God lead the goals — and He'll lead the results."

January 31 —
When Excellence Becomes Influence

"Let us not love with words or speech but with actions and in truth."
— 1 John 3:18

Eventually, excellence stops being something you *do* — it becomes something you *are*. Over time, consistency builds identity, identity builds reputation, and reputation builds influence. People stop following your instructions and start following your example.

Real influence isn't gifted — it's earned. It is forged through reliability, humility, integrity, and performance over time. When people trust your character and respect your work ethic, they willingly follow your leadership.

Excellence becomes influence when your actions do the talking.

Reflection Questions

1. Is my example strong enough that others are motivated to follow it voluntarily?

2. What area of my leadership most needs consistency?

Author Quote — Coach David Angeron

"When your actions speak clearly enough, leadership becomes effortless."

FEBRUARY

LEADERSHIP, DISCIPLINE & EXECUTION

February 1 — Discipline Beats Talent

"The hand of the diligent will rule." — Proverbs 12:24

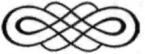

Talent can take you places — but without discipline, you won't stay there. Talent gives you a head start; discipline determines the finish line. It's easy to work hard when energy is high, applause is loud, and progress is visible. But true discipline shows up on the days when motivation has vanished and results feel distant. Discipline is doing what needs to be done even when you don't feel like doing it. It is a commitment to consistency, not convenience.

Many of the greatest leaders, athletes, and entrepreneurs weren't the most naturally gifted — they were simply committed to daily habits most people refuse to maintain. God doesn't multiply wishful thinking — He multiplies diligent action. Effort, repetition, and follow-through activate potential. You don't need to pray for more talent; you need to steward the talent you already have with elite consistency. The leaders who change the world are not always the most gifted… but they are always the most disciplined.

Reflection Questions

1. Where have I been leaning too heavily on talent instead of discipline?

2. What daily discipline would radically upgrade my leadership over time?

Author Quote — Coach David Angeron

"Talent may set the bar — but discipline determines who clears it."

February 2 —
Small Habits, Big Harvest

Success is not built in a single moment — it is built in a thousand small moments done with intention. Most people overestimate what big actions will do once in a while and underestimate what small actions will do every single day. Daily habits are like seeds: some look tiny and unimpressive at first, yet over time they produce extraordinary harvests. The person who builds small but powerful habits eventually experiences growth that looks "overnight" to everyone else — but it wasn't luck; it was consistency.

Whether it's reading daily, saving a percentage of income, speaking life into your team, or praying every morning, small disciplines reshape your future one day at a time. Change doesn't require perfection — just consistency. Leaders who honor the small things eventually become trusted with the big things. If you want a big harvest, plant small habits now and refuse to stop watering them.

Reflection Questions

1. What is one small daily habit I can adopt that would produce big results over time?

2. What unproductive habit needs to be replaced immediately?

Author Quote — Coach David Angeron

"Greatness is just small habits stacked consistently over time."

February 3 — Vision With Clarity

"Write the vision; make it plain." — Habakkuk 2:2

A mbition is not leadership — clarity is. Many organizations have incredible dreams but unclear direction. A vision can be inspiring but still confusing if it is not communicated simply and repeatedly. A team cannot pursue what it cannot clearly understand. When vision is vague, frustration rises, motivation fades, and productivity stalls. But when the vision is clear — where we're going, why it matters, and what success looks like — momentum becomes natural.

Clarity eliminates wasted effort. It aligns every meeting, every strategy, and every decision. People are willing to work hard when they know the mission is meaningful. When team members understand the "why," they serve with passion rather than pressure. A clear vision unites talent and energy toward one purpose — and when that happens, the ordinary becomes unstoppable. A leader's job is not just to have vision — but to communicate vision until it burns in the hearts of the people.

Reflection Questions

1. Is the vision of my organization or team clearly communicated and repeatable?

2. Can the people I lead explain the "why" behind our mission?

Author Quote — Coach David Angeron

"A vision people can't understand is a vision people can't run after."

FEBRUARY 4 — HARD CONVERSATIONS, HEALTHY COMPANIES

"Speak the truth in love." — Ephesians 4:15

Leadership is not just celebration — it is confrontation. Avoiding difficult conversations protects feelings temporarily but damages the culture permanently. Feedback is not unkind; silence is. When teams don't address issues early, disrespect grows, resentment spreads, and excellence weakens. Healthy organizations deal with conflict before conflict deals with them.

Correction done with empathy is a gift — it protects potential, clarifies expectations, and restores alignment. A leader can love someone deeply and still hold them accountable. Comfort-based leadership creates weak cultures; truth-based leadership creates strong ones. Difficult conversations are never fun, but they are always necessary. A great leader would rather experience a moment of discomfort than manage years of dysfunction.

Reflection Questions

1. Which difficult conversation am I avoiding, and why?

2. How can I communicate accountability with love and respect?

Author Quote — Coach David Angeron

"Tough conversations don't hurt teams — avoiding them does."

February 5 —
Do What Others Won't

Greatness isn't a mystery — it's a pattern. Extraordinary success follows ordinary moments of discipline repeated when others choose ease. Everyone wants success until they see what it requires. The leaders who rise are the ones willing to stretch farther, learn deeper, and serve wider than the average person. While others wait for opportunity, they prepare for it. While others look for recognition, they look for responsibility.

The marketplace doesn't reward the comfortable — it rewards the committed. Excellence will always require decisions others avoid: showing up early, staying late, having humility, taking initiative, and doing the small things no one celebrates. God elevates leaders who embrace service, sacrifice, and stewardship. If you want uncommon results, you must embrace an uncommon work ethic and attitude.

Reflection Questions

1. Where am I operating like everyone else instead of doing what separates me?

2. What "extra mile" decision can I make today?

Author Quote — Coach David Angeron

"Leaders who do what others won't achieve what others can't."

February 6 —
Building Systems, Not Stress

Hard work is not the problem — disorganized work is. Many leaders don't burn out because of workload but because of lack of structure. When planning, delegation, and workflows are absent, everything requires effort, urgency, and emotional energy. Systems create order, and order creates peace. When systems are in place, excellence becomes predictable instead of exhausting.

Systems don't eliminate work — they eliminate chaos. They protect time, attention, consistency, and culture. From automated reminders to checklists, scheduling tools, onboarding frameworks, customer scripts, and weekly structure — systems allow organizations to grow without draining the leaders who built them. You should not have to sacrifice your health to see progress. Build models that carry the weight so you can focus on mission instead of micromanagement.

Reflection Questions

1. Where do I need a system instead of more effort?
2. Which tasks should be automated, delegated, or scheduled?

Author Quote — Coach David Angeron

"Leaders build organizations that run on systems — not stress."

FEBRUARY 7 — RADICAL OWNERSHIP

"Each of us will give an account of ourselves to God." — Romans 14:12

Leadership isn't about assigning blame — it's about taking responsibility. Progress stops the moment excuses start. Radical ownership means refusing to look outward before looking inward. It means identifying your part in the problem so you can become part of the solution. It doesn't mean every issue is your fault — it means every issue is your responsibility to respond to.

When leaders embrace ownership, accountability becomes empowering rather than intimidating. Mistakes turn into lessons. Failures turn into data. Pressure turns into fuel for improvement. The leaders who rise are the ones who stop defending their weaknesses and start transforming them. Ownership accelerates growth — excuses prolong stagnation. You will never fix what you continue to justify.

Reflection Questions

1. Where am I making excuses instead of taking responsibility?

2. What failure or weakness can I transform into a leadership win?

Author Quote — Coach David Angeron

"You can complain about results or take ownership of them — you cannot do both."

February 8 — Planning for Multiplication

"Be fruitful and multiply." — Genesis 1:28

Leaders are not called to manage blessings — but to multiply them. Addition is doing more yourself; multiplication is empowering more people to do meaningful work with you. Many leaders stay overwhelmed because everything depends on their hands. Multiplication requires letting go of control, elevating others, and building systems that outlive your personal capacity.

Multiplying leaders means developing, trusting, training, and delegating — not hoarding authority. A healthy organization doesn't rely on one superstar — it equips dozens. Multiplication is not just about income, scale, or opportunities — it is about impact that expands beyond the leader. It's not success if it dies when you stop touching it. Build something that grows stronger even in your absence.

Reflection Questions

1. Am I building for addition or multiplication?

2. Who can I develop into a stronger leader this month?

Author Quote — Coach David Angeron

"Multiplication begins when leaders stop trying to do everything and start developing everyone."

45

FEBRUARY 9 — LONG-GAME LEADERSHIP

"Let us run with endurance the race that is set before us." — Hebrews 12:1

Anyone can lead when progress is fast and applause is loud — but legacy leadership requires endurance. We live in a world addicted to instant gratification, overnight success, and quick rewards. But in reality, the most meaningful results require months and years of consistency. Leadership is not about speed — it's about stamina.

Every setback is not a sign of failure — it's a test of commitment. Every delay is not denial — sometimes it's development. God builds leaders the way He builds mountains: slowly, layer by layer, challenge by challenge, season by season. So don't resent the wait — respect it. The habits you sustain today will support the platform God brings tomorrow.

Reflection Questions

1. Where have I been expecting instant results instead of long-term growth?

2. What area of leadership requires more patience and persistence?

Author Quote — Coach David Angeron

"Anyone can start fast — only leaders finish faithfully."

February 10 — Speed With Strategy

Speed can grow a business — but speed without strategy can destroy one. Many leaders operate in constant motion but limited progress. Activity feels like achievement until resources are wasted, teams are exhausted, and momentum turns into chaos. Fast isn't powerful — *focused fast* is. Strategy is the difference between movement and progress.

Strategic speed requires counsel, research, planning, timing, and risk assessment. It means asking wise questions before racing toward execution. When direction is clear, speed is an advantage. When direction is absent, speed becomes costly. Leaders don't just ask, "How fast can we go?" They ask, "How far will this take us?"

Reflection Questions

1. What decision have I been rushing that requires more strategy?

2. Who do I need to seek wisdom or feedback from before proceeding?

Author Quote — Coach David Angeron

"Speed grows a business — strategy sustains it."

FEBRUARY 11 — THE ROI OF REST

"He makes me lie down in green pastures." — Psalm 23:2

Rest is not a reward — it is a requirement. In God's design for humanity, rest came before exhaustion. Before sin, before stress, before deadlines — there was rest. That means rest is not a sign of weakness; it is part of worship. Leaders often push themselves past healthy limits because they associate constant work with loyalty and success. But an overworked leader eventually becomes an ineffective leader. Rest sharpens judgment, deepens creativity, rebuilds emotional capacity, and restores spiritual strength. When a leader ignores rest, everything they influence eventually suffers — their family, team, health, clarity, and character.

Leadership success isn't measured only by what you can push through — but by how well you can steward your energy for longevity. Your assignment requires you healthy, not just hardworking. When you rest, you're not quitting — you're preparing to come back stronger. Recovery isn't the pause between productivity... it's part of the productivity.

Reflection Questions

1. Do I see rest as part of leadership or as the opposite of it?

2. What rhythms of rest do I need to schedule — not wait for?

Author Quote — Coach David Angeron

"Rest isn't retreat — it's refuel."

February 12 —
The Power of Follow-Through

Vision is inspiring — but follow-through is influential. Anyone can start something with excitement; few finish with consistency. Teams, employees, customers, family members, and investors judge a leader less by emotion and more by execution. A leader's reliability builds trust, and trust builds momentum. Every promise kept reinforces confidence in your leadership; every promise abandoned makes confidence harder to give next time.

Follow-through isn't about perfection — it's about intentionality. It requires discipline to stay focused, time management to protect priorities, and integrity to honor your word even when feelings change. Leadership grows not by the volume of commitments we make but by the consistency of commitments we fulfill. Passion motivates the start — character finishes the assignment. The world doesn't need more ambitious starters... it needs dependable finishers.

Reflection Questions

1. Where have I been starting more than I finish?

2. Which commitment needs immediate completion this week?

Author Quote — Coach David Angeron

"Your greatest leadership skill is not what you promise — it's what you finish."

FEBRUARY 13 — ELIMINATE EXCUSES

"All hard work brings a profit, but mere talk leads only to poverty."
— Proverbs 14:23

Excuses are comfortable — but they are costly. They sound reasonable, justified, and even noble at times, yet they quietly rob leaders of progress, influence, and momentum. Excuses don't make life easier — they make growth slower. Every excuse protects feelings in the moment but destroys potential over time. Leaders who remove excuses unlock possibility. They stop waiting for perfect timing, ideal resources, or complete clarity. They decide that forward is better than flawless.

An excuse-free leader is not a leader with perfect conditions — it's a leader with a determined mindset. Instead of defending what limits them, they confront it. Instead of resenting challenges, they look for solutions. Instead of sitting still, they take the next step. God can multiply action — but He cannot multiply excuses. Nothing changes until responsibility replaces rationalization.

Reflection Questions

1. What excuse has been holding me back the most?

2. What action can I take immediately to replace excuses with execution?

Author Quote — Coach David Angeron

"Excuses build walls — action builds outcomes."

February 14 — Make Love a Leadership Strategy

"Do everything in love." — 1 Corinthians 16:14

Love is the greatest competitive advantage in leadership — not softness, not weakness, not emotionalism, but love rooted in honor and value for people. Teams don't thrive in environments filled with pressure, fear, and criticism; they thrive in environments filled with respect, support, encouragement, and truth. Love elevates expectations while still providing compassion. It celebrates wins, develops potential, and corrects dysfunction without devaluing the person.

Love doesn't remove accountability — it makes accountability meaningful. When people know they are cared for, instruction feels like investment rather than insult. Love turns leadership from positional authority into relational influence. When people feel loved by leadership, they don't just complete tasks — they fight for the mission. They don't just stay — they grow. They don't just serve — they belong.

Reflection Questions

1. Has my leadership felt more demanding than compassionate lately?

2. Who needs encouragement, affirmation, or grace from me today?

Author Quote — Coach David Angeron

"You can lead people by authority — but you transform them by love."

February 15 — Accountability Accelerates Growth

Accountability is not a threat to leadership — it is protection for it. Leaders without accountability may gain progress quickly, but they lose direction quietly. Blind spots go uncorrected, weaknesses go unchallenged, and patterns go unnoticed. No leader rises to their full potential in isolation. Accountability provides feedback, insight, support, correction, wisdom, and perspective that a leader cannot generate alone.

Humility is the doorway to accountability. It takes maturity to listen, courage to receive correction, and strength to invite challenge. Accountability doesn't expose failure — it prevents it. It turns potential into excellence and character into credibility. Without accountability, leaders plateau; with it, leaders grow. The difference between leaders who remain average and leaders who excel is not talent — it is teachability.

Reflection Questions

1. Do I invite accountability or avoid it?

2. Who have I given permission to tell me the truth even when it's uncomfortable?

Author Quote — Coach David Angeron

"Accountability isn't control — it's a gift that unlocks greatness."

February 16 — A Leader's Routine

"Teach us to number our days, that we may gain a heart of wisdom."
— Psalm 90:12

Your habits preach louder than your words. Every day, your routine is forming your leadership — whether intentionally or accidentally. Successful leaders don't wait for motivation to show up; they build rhythms that carry them even when motivation fades. Time follows priority when priority is scheduled. Without structure, urgent things suffocate important things — and life becomes reactive instead of purposeful.

A strong routine doesn't just include work — it protects faith, rest, growth, and relationships. When the calendar supports your calling, your calling becomes sustainable. It's not about cramming more into the day — it's about designing the day around what matters most. You cannot lead with wisdom if your life is organized around randomness.

Reflection Questions

1. Does my current routine reflect my priorities and calling?

2. What habit needs to be added — and what distraction needs to be removed?

Author Quote — Coach David Angeron

"You don't rise to the level of your goals — you fall to the level of your routines."

FEBRUARY 17 —
PROTECTING YOUR MINDSET

"Do not conform to the pattern of this world, but be transformed by the renewing of your mind." — Romans 12:2

Mindset is the steering wheel of leadership. Skills matter, strategy matters, talent matters — but mindset determines direction. A strong mind produces strong leadership; an unguarded mind produces inconsistency, insecurity, and instability. The enemy knows that if he can corrupt a leader's thinking, he can derail their calling. That's why protecting your mind is not optional — it's warfare.

What you repeatedly hear and think becomes what you eventually believe. Garbage in creates doubt, fear, and burnout. God's Word in creates confidence, peace, resilience, and clarity. Surrounding yourself with negativity is a choice — so is surrounding yourself with growth. Great leaders curate what they consume and who they allow to influence them.

Reflection Questions

1. What consistently drains my mindset — and why do I allow it?

2. What environment or content do I need more of to protect my focus?

Author Quote — Coach David Angeron

"You cannot build a strong life with a weak mindset — guard your mind like your calling depends on it, because it does."

February 18 —
Excellence in Everything

"Do everything for the glory of God." — 1 Corinthians 10:31

Excellence is not a standard for special occasions — it is a lifestyle of leadership. It is the choice to give your best not because someone is checking, but because God is watching. Excellence honors God and inspires people. It communicates value, consistency, and reliability. When you approach small tasks with big commitment, opportunities begin to expand.

Excellence is not perfection — it is intentionality. It's showing up prepared, following through with quality, treating every assignment as ministry, and producing work that reflects your integrity. God promotes leaders who are faithful in "little things" long before He puts them over big things. The path to influence is paved with excellence long before recognition arrives.

Reflection Questions

1. What area of my life have I been treating as "small" instead of giving it excellence?

2. How would my leadership change if every task became worship?

Author Quote — Coach David Angeron

"Excellence isn't a performance — it's a lifestyle."

February 19 — Winning Without Burning Out

G od never asked you to sacrifice your health, your family, or your peace on the altar of success. Winning at work while losing at home is not winning. Leading well while destroying your soul is not leadership. Burnout doesn't come from doing too much — it comes from doing too much disconnected from God and your core priorities.

You can chase goals and still protect what matters. You can be driven without being drained. You can pursue excellence without sacrificing emotional health. When a leader works from rest instead of working for rest, leadership becomes sustainable. Success should add to your life — not take your life from you. Long-term impact requires long-term health.

Reflection Questions

1. Am I chasing success in a way that's hurting my health, family, or faith?

2. What boundaries would allow me to win without burning out?

Author Quote — Coach David Angeron

"Success without sustainability becomes self-destruction — win in a way you can keep winning."

FEBRUARY 20
— DISTRACTIONS DESTROY DESTINY

"A double-minded man is unstable in all his ways." — James 1:8

Greatness is rarely lost through major failures — but often through minor distractions. The enemy doesn't always need to attack leaders directly; he only needs to divide their focus. When attention is scattered, purpose slowly fades. Every yes given to distraction becomes a no given to calling. Leaders don't drown in lack of opportunity — they drown in lack of focus.

Distractions are dangerous because they often feel harmless, normal, or even urgent. But anything that consistently steals energy, time, or clarity becomes a silent assassin of destiny. Protecting your assignment requires eliminating noise, simplifying priorities, and guarding your attention like it's treasure — because it is. The future belongs to the focused.

Reflection Questions

1. What distraction has been stealing my focus and momentum?

2. Where do I need to replace attention with intention?

Author Quote — Coach David Angeron

"Distractions don't always look dangerous — but they are always expensive."

February 21 — Show Up Prepared

Preparation is not about perfection — it's about stewardship. When you walk into meetings, opportunities, assignments, or conversations prepared, you communicate strength, excellence, hunger, and respect. It shows that you value the people you're serving, the mission you're building, and the God who opened the door in the first place. Far too many talented people rely on gifting while neglecting preparation — and it costs them influence. Talent can get you noticed, but preparation keeps you trusted.

God often tests leaders privately with preparation before He promotes them publicly with opportunity. If you only show up ready when the platform is big, you will likely never reach the platform at all. Prepared leaders don't rise on accident — they rise on purpose. They study, rehearse, practice, plan, and cultivate discipline long before anyone sees the results. The leaders who grow the fastest are not always the most gifted — just the most prepared.

Reflection Questions

1. Where have I been showing up with talent but not preparation?

2. What habit of preparation would immediately raise my performance?

Author Quote — Coach David Angeron

"You can't ask God to bless opportunities you haven't prepared for."

FEBRUARY 22 —
LEADERSHIP VS. MANAGEMENT

"The greatest among you will be your servant." — Matthew 23:11

Management and leadership both matter — but they are not the same. Management maintains what already exists; leadership builds what doesn't exist yet. Management keeps systems functional; leadership keeps people growing. Organizations need management to run — but they need leadership to rise. A team can be well-managed and still stagnant if no one is leading it toward transformation.

Leaders don't just ask, "What needs to get done?" They ask, "Who do we need to become to fulfill our mission?" Leadership requires vision for the future, wisdom for the present, and courage to challenge comfort. It prioritizes developing people over merely accomplishing tasks. You can manage without inspiring — but you cannot lead without serving. The true measure of leadership isn't control, titles, or busyness — it's multiplied impact through others.

Reflection Questions

1. Am I spending too much time managing tasks and not enough time developing people?

2. What leadership habit can replace a maintenance habit?

Author Quote — Coach David Angeron

"Management keeps things running — leadership keeps things rising."

FEBRUARY 23 —
CONFIDENCE WITHOUT EGO

"Therefore, do not throw away your confidence; it will be richly rewarded."
— Hebrews 10:35

Confidence and humility are not opposites — they are teammates. Confidence without humility becomes arrogance, and humility without confidence becomes insecurity. God calls leaders to walk boldly while bowing low. Confidence honors God when it comes from your identity in Him, not from pride in yourself. Ego says, "I am the source." True confidence says, "God is the source, and He equipped me."

Leaders who lack confidence shrink back from opportunity and impact. Leaders who lack humility damage culture and repel people. The strongest leaders walk into rooms knowing they belong there — not because they are great, but because God placed them there. They carry authority without entitlement, strength without superiority, and boldness without disrespect. Confidence wins rooms — humility wins hearts — and together they change organizations.

Reflection Questions

1. Am I hiding behind false humility, or am I stepping boldly into what God called me to do?

2. Where can I practice confidence and humility today?

Author Quote — Coach David Angeron

"Confidence wins rooms — humility wins hearts."

February 24 —
Leadership Requires Self-Control

"Better a patient person than a warrior, one with self-control than one who takes a city." — Proverbs 16:32

A leader's greatest enemy is often not the competition — but their own impulses. Power without self-control becomes destructive. Influence without restraint becomes dangerous. Self-control is not emotionless leadership; it is disciplined leadership. It is the ability to respond instead of react, to pause instead of explode, to choose wisdom over impulse. A leader who cannot manage their emotions eventually damages their credibility and their culture.

As leaders grow in responsibility, the demand for emotional maturity increases. People follow leaders they can depend on — not leaders who are unpredictable, reactive, or unstable. Self-control doesn't mean denying emotion; it means directing emotion. Even Jesus experienced anger — but He expressed it with purpose, not rage. Greatness doesn't require the absence of feelings — but the mastery of them.

Reflection Questions

1. Which emotion or impulse do I most need to get control of?

2. When pressure hits, do I react emotionally or respond intentionally?

Author Quote — Coach David Angeron

"Great leaders don't deny emotion — they discipline it."

FEBRUARY 25 —
BE BETTER THAN YESTERDAY

"But one thing I do: forgetting what is behind and straining toward what is ahead."
— Philippians 3:13

The only person you must be better than is the person you were yesterday. The world teaches us to compare our progress to others — but God calls us to grow according to the potential He placed inside us. Comparison creates insecurity and jealousy; continuous improvement creates maturity and momentum. Growth isn't measured by how fast you advance — but by how intentionally you advance.

You don't need to transform everything at once — just improve something today. Learn something new. Strengthen a weakness. Practice a skill. Honor God in one new area. It doesn't matter how small the step is, as long as the step is forward. When growth becomes your daily goal, success becomes inevitable. Consistency compounds — and so does improvement.

Reflection Questions

1. In what area do I need to make a 1% improvement today?

2. Where have I been comparing myself instead of improving myself?

Author Quote — Coach David Angeron

"Success isn't beating others — it's outgrowing who you were."

February 26 — Consistency Creates Momentum

Momentum doesn't appear suddenly — it is built slowly. Every small act of discipline adds fuel to the fire of progress. Most people wait for motivation to begin — but leaders take action consistently, and motivation follows afterward. Once consistency emerges, pressure shrinks and progress increases. Excellence becomes predictable, not painful.

Intensity can produce a great day — but consistency produces a great life. The scoreboard of leadership is not measured by how big you start, but by how long you continue. When you master consistency, you become unstoppable because your progress is not dependent on feelings, applause, or convenience. Success is not a moment — it's a pattern.

Reflection Questions

1. Where do I start strong but fail to stay consistent?

2. What doable daily action will build the momentum I need?

Author Quote — Coach David Angeron

"Momentum isn't luck — it's consistency multiplied over time."

FEBRUARY 27 — SELF-AWARENESS OVER SELF-IMPORTANCE

Self-awareness is one of the greatest superpowers in leadership. You cannot grow beyond what you refuse to acknowledge. Self-importance blinds leaders to their weaknesses, while self-awareness exposes growth opportunities. A leader who is teachable, reflective, and honest will always outgrow a leader who is gifted but prideful.

Self-awareness doesn't lower confidence — it protects it. It helps you understand strengths and stretch them, acknowledge weaknesses and improve them, and identify blind spots before they become problems. Leaders who seek feedback don't lose authority — they strengthen it. Asking for help is not a weakness — it is wisdom. The greatest leaders are students before they are experts.

Reflection Questions

1. What weakness or blind spot have I been avoiding?

2. Who can help me see what I don't recognize on my own?

Author Quote — Coach David Angeron

"Great leaders aren't perfect — they're self-aware and always improving."

February 28 — Where Focus Goes, Growth Happens

Your focus is one of the most valuable assets you steward. Whatever captures your attention shapes your future. You cannot grow in an area you continually neglect. You cannot rise in an area you repeatedly ignore. Focus is not accidental — it is intentional and protected. Every day you are training your mind to choose what matters and reject what doesn't.

Growth accelerates when priorities get clarity. Ask: What deserves my attention? What does not deserve my attention? Sometimes the biggest breakthrough does not require new effort — only new focus. You don't need more hours in the day — you need fewer distractions in the day. When a leader learns to direct their focus, they unlock their future.

Reflection Questions

1. What has received too much of my focus lately?

2. What single priority deserves my focus this week?

Author Quote — Coach David Angeron

"You can't grow what you won't focus on."

February 29 — Intentional Leaders, Intentional Companies

Nothing great is built by accident. Intentional leadership creates intentional culture, and intentional culture creates intentional results. When leaders operate reactively instead of proactively, the organization becomes directionless. But when leaders think deliberately, schedule strategically, and execute consistently, excellence becomes automatic instead of accidental.

Intentionality requires discipline, clarity, planning, structure, and purpose-driven decisions. It means designing outcomes instead of hoping for them. It means creating habits that reinforce values, not contradict them. As the leader becomes intentional, the team becomes intentional — and when the team becomes intentional, the company becomes unstoppable. Success becomes sustainable because it is built on strategy, not luck.

Reflection Questions

1. Which area of my leadership has been accidental instead of intentional?

2. What specific intentional change can I start today?

Author Quote — Coach David Angeron

"What you build intentionally — you won't lose accidentally."

MARCH

RELATIONSHIPS, TEAM BUILDING & CULTURE

MARCH 1 — CULTURE IS THE COMPANY

"Every kingdom divided against itself will be ruined." — Matthew 12:25

Culture is not a side topic — it *is* the company. Products can be copied, marketing can be mimicked, and strategies can be studied. But culture is unique because it's built daily by the values, behaviors, and attitudes that leaders allow. It determines whether people are simply clocking in or carrying a sense of calling. Toxic cultures drain energy, divide teams, and eventually destroy potential — even if the product is great. Healthy cultures attract talent, keep loyalty high, and multiply impact.

Culture is shaped by:
- What leaders reward
- What leaders tolerate
- How leaders communicate
- How leaders treat people

Every policy, meeting, decision, and conversation either builds culture or breaks it down. The leader's attitude becomes the organization's atmosphere. You cannot expect a championship performance from a dysfunctional environment. If you want a winning team, you must intentionally design a winning culture — on purpose, every single day.

Reflection Questions

1. What behaviors am I tolerating that weaken culture?
2. What does a winning culture look like in my organization?

Author Quote — Coach David Angeron

"Culture is not what you say — it's what you allow."

MARCH 2 — PEOPLE OVER PROFITS

"Do to others as you would have them do to you." — Luke 6:31

Profit is important for sustainability — but people are essential for purpose. An organization that prioritizes profit at the expense of people may grow fast, but it will not grow healthy. When people feel used, they eventually disengage, resist, or leave. When people feel valued, they bring creativity, loyalty, and extra effort that no paycheck alone can buy. People are not interruptions to your work — they *are* the work.

When leaders see people as image-bearers of God, not tools for production, everything changes. Conversations become more respectful, expectations become clearer, and decisions consider impact beyond the bottom line. Honor, empathy, fairness, and real appreciation create environments where people want to stay and contribute. Ironically, when you prioritize people, profit often increases — because people who feel valued give their best.

Reflection Questions

1. Am I valuing people as highly as I value results?

2. How can I show appreciation and support to my team this week?

Author Quote — Coach David Angeron

"When leaders put people first, people give their best."

MARCH 3 —

HIRING FOR HEART AND HUNGER

"Man looks at the outward appearance, but the Lord looks at the heart."
— 1 Samuel 16:7

Resumes can reveal skills, but they can't fully reveal spirit. Experience can show where someone has been, but not always where they're willing to go. That's why wise leaders look beyond qualifications to heart and hunger. A highly skilled person with a bad attitude can damage culture faster than they add value. A teachable, hungry person with solid character can grow quickly and become a long-term asset.

Hire people who:
- ♦ Take initiative
- ♦ Stay humble
- ♦ Crave growth
- ♦ Add energy, not drama
- ♦ Serve the mission, not themselves

You can train skills with time and coaching, but you cannot train integrity, humility, or drive. Heart determines how someone shows up when no one is watching. Hunger determines how fast they develop once they're given opportunity. Build teams filled with the right heart and relentless hunger, and performance, innovation, and culture will follow.

Reflection Questions

1. Have I been evaluating talent while ignoring character or attitude?
2. What qualities matter most for protecting and elevating our culture?

Author Quote — Coach David Angeron

"It's easier to teach skills than to fix character — hire accordingly."

March 4 — Unity Wins Championships

Talent can fill a roster — unity fills a trophy case. A team full of gifted people will still lose if they're secretly competing with each other, undermining decisions, or guarding their own ego. Unity doesn't mean sameness; it means shared mission. It means people are willing to sacrifice personal spotlight for collective success. When hearts are united around purpose, diversity of perspective becomes an advantage instead of a wedge.

Unity multiplies strength. It creates trust, speeds up communication, and allows teams to act as one. Division, on the other hand, drains energy and magnifies small issues into major conflicts. Protecting unity means addressing offenses quickly, clarifying expectations, and reminding everyone regularly who we are and why we're here. When unity is strong, pressure pulls people together instead of pulling them apart.

Reflection Questions

1. Is my team aligned around mission — or around personal preferences?

2. What conversations, values, or boundaries are needed to strengthen unity?

Author Quote — Coach David Angeron

"Talent may win games — but unity wins championships."

MARCH 5 —
THE POWER OF TRUST CAPITAL

"Whoever can be trusted with little can also be trusted with much." — Luke 16:10

Trust is the most powerful form of capital a leader can possess. You can have title, authority, and expertise — but if people don't trust you, they will comply without truly committing. Trust is what turns instructions into inspiration and policies into passion. It is formed not in grand gestures, but in everyday consistency.

Trust is built through:

♦ Consistency — doing what you say over time
♦ Transparency — being honest about challenges and decisions
♦ Reliability — showing up when it matters most
♦ Accountability — owning mistakes instead of hiding them

When trust is high, teams move quickly, adapt well, and communicate openly. When trust is low, everything slows down because people doubt motives and question decisions. As a leader, every action either deposits into or withdraws from your trust account. Guard it. Grow it. Steward it well.

Reflection Questions

1. What decisions or habits can I change to build more trust with my team?

2. Do people see me as reliable — or unpredictable?

Author Quote — Coach David Angeron

"When trust rises, everything else rises with it."

MARCH 6 — COMMUNICATION BUILDS OR BREAKS TEAMS

"Let your conversation be always full of grace." — Colossians 4:6

Communication is more than words — it's leadership in motion. Teams don't usually fall apart because of lack of talent; they fall apart because of lack of clarity. When people don't know what's expected, what's changing, or what matters most, frustration grows. Silence gets filled with assumptions, and assumptions rarely lean positive.

Great communication is:

♦ Clear — people know exactly what is meant
♦ Timely — people hear things before it's too late
♦ Honest — truth is not hidden or twisted
♦ Respectful — dignity is preserved
♦ Strategic — the right people hear the right message

Communication either aligns or divides, energizes or confuses. As a leader, you are always communicating — even when you're not talking. Your nonverbal cues, responsiveness, and transparency all send messages. Don't wait for miscommunication to create chaos. Say what needs to be said, with grace and courage.

Reflection Questions

1. Does my communication provide clarity — or create confusion?

2. What conversation do I need to have to strengthen alignment?

Author Quote — Coach David Angeron

"Your culture will rise or fall to the level of your communication."

March 7 —
The Right People Raise the Bar

You are never just working *around* people — you are becoming more like them. Attitudes, disciplines, and standards are contagious. Spend enough time with people who complain, coast, and compromise, and your own standards begin to slip. But surround yourself with people who strive, sacrifice, and grow, and your capacity increases.

The right people:

♦ Challenge your excuses
♦ Celebrate your progress
♦ Call you higher when you settle
♦ Model what excellence looks like daily

If you feel stuck, check your circle. Sometimes your environment is lowering your ceiling. The people you work closest with should not just be compatible — they should be catalytic. Great leaders intentionally build inner circles that stretch them, sharpen them, and call out their best. When the bar is high around you, it becomes natural to rise.

Reflection Questions

1. Do the people closest to me elevate or lower my standards?

2. Who sharpens me — and who softens my drive?

Author Quote — Coach David Angeron

"The right people don't compete with you — they sharpen you."

March 8 — Replace Gossip With Gratitude

Gossip doesn't just talk about people — it tears them down. It erodes trust, fuels division, and slowly ruins culture. When gossip is tolerated, people spend their energy criticizing instead of creating, complaining instead of contributing. Leaders cannot allow this poison to spread and then wonder why unity is weak.

The antidote to gossip is gratitude. Where gossip hunts for flaws, gratitude highlights strengths. Gratitude creates a culture where people feel seen, valued, and honored. It shifts conversations from "What's wrong with them?" to "What's right about them?" As a leader, you set the tone: you shut gossip down with courage and redirect it with honor.

Speak life. Celebrate effort. Publicly recognize growth. The more gratitude flows, the less room there is for gossip to survive.

Reflection Questions

1. Where has gossip been tolerated or ignored in my environment?

2. Who on my team deserves appreciation rather than criticism?

Author Quote — Coach David Angeron

"Gossip kills culture — gratitude builds it."

March 9 — Protecting Culture at All Costs

Just like the heart determines the life of the body, culture determines the life of the organization. Culture is precious — and fragile. It's easier to protect than to repair. The moment you compromise on core values, culture begins to erode. What you overlook today becomes the norm tomorrow.

Protect culture by:

- ♦ Rewarding the right behaviors
- ♦ Correcting the wrong ones immediately
- ♦ Removing toxicity without hesitation

This requires courage. It means having hard conversations, making difficult personnel decisions, and refusing to tolerate attitudes or actions that poison the environment — even if the person is productive. Great culture is not accidental; it is guarded. When leaders protect culture, they protect the long-term health, reputation, and impact of the organization.

Reflection Questions

1. Where have I avoided protecting culture because it was uncomfortable?

2. What behavior needs to be addressed or eliminated immediately?

Author Quote — Coach David Angeron

"If you don't protect culture, you will eventually pay for culture."

MARCH 10 — SERVING WHILE LEADING

Jesus redefined leadership forever. He showed that true greatness is not found in how many people serve you, but in how many people you serve. Leadership is not a throne — it's a towel and a basin. It's influence used for the good of others, not the comfort of self. Serving doesn't weaken your authority; it deepens it.

Servant leadership means you:

♦ Elevate others, not just yourself
♦ Coach, mentor, and develop people
♦ Help remove obstacles from their path
♦ Combine high standards with high support

It doesn't mean lowering expectations or avoiding difficult conversations. In fact, serving people often means expecting more from them because you see more *in* them. When people know you are for them, they let you challenge them. When they feel supported, they respond with effort, loyalty, and ownership.

Reflection Questions

1. Do I view leadership as service or status?
2. How can I invest more intentionally in the people I lead?

Author Quote — Coach David Angeron

"Leadership isn't about being lifted above others — it's about lifting others higher."

March 11 — Encourage in Public, Correct in Private

"Therefore encourage one another and build each other up."
— 1 Thessalonians 5:11

The way you deliver praise and correction matters as much as the message itself. Public encouragement multiplies morale, energy, and confidence. When people see others honored, it reinforces what is valued and celebrated. Public correction, however, often creates shame, defensiveness, and quiet resentment. It may get quick compliance, but it wounds trust.

Wise leaders understand this pattern:

- ◆ Encourage in public to inspire the team
- ◆ Correct in private to protect dignity

That doesn't mean avoiding hard feedback — it means delivering it in the right setting and the right spirit. When feedback is given privately, with clarity and care, people are more likely to receive it as development instead of an attack. Build a culture where celebration is loud and common, and where correction is honest but handled with honor.

Reflection Questions

1. Do I praise loudly and correct respectfully?
2. Who deserves public encouragement this week?

Author Quote — Coach David Angeron

"Correct in private to protect dignity — honor in public to build morale."

March 12 — Healthy Teams Handle Tension

Tension is inevitable where passion exists. Any team made up of driven, opinionated, gifted people will experience disagreements. The difference between weak teams and strong teams is not the absence of conflict — it's how they handle it. Avoidance feels easier in the moment but far more costly long-term.

Unhealthy teams:

♦ Avoid hard conversations
♦ Let resentment quietly grow
♦ Vent instead of resolving

Healthy teams:

♦ Talk about issues directly
♦ Listen fully before responding
♦ Focus on solutions, not blame

Tension handled with humility, honesty, and respect actually strengthens trust. It shows that relationships are strong enough to handle truth. As a leader, your response to tension teaches everyone else how to respond. Don't fear it — steward it.

Reflection Questions

1. Have I been avoiding an uncomfortable conversation instead of resolving it?

2. How can I model maturity during moments of tension?

Author Quote — Coach David Angeron

"Conflict doesn't break strong teams — silence does."

MARCH 13 — LOYALTY WITH ACCOUNTABILITY

Real loyalty doesn't just clap for you — it corrects you. It doesn't just protect your feelings — it protects your future. Many leaders confuse loyalty with blind agreement, but that's not loyalty; that's passivity. Genuine loyalty is willing to risk temporary discomfort to protect long-term growth.

Accountability without loyalty feels harsh and critical. Loyalty without accountability feels shallow and weak. Together, they create relationships that sharpen, strengthen, and stretch people into who God designed them to be. Great teams are made up of people who tell each other the truth, even when it stings — and they do it with love, honor, and humility.

As a leader, be loyal enough to correct, and humble enough to be corrected.

Reflection Questions

1. Do I avoid accountability because I fear losing loyalty?

2. Who needs truth from me — spoken with love?

Author Quote — Coach David Angeron

"Loyalty celebrates you — accountability sharpens you."

MARCH 14 —
CONFLICT ISN'T THE ENEMY

Peace is powerful — but peace is not the same as pretending. Many leaders mistake the absence of visible conflict for health, when in reality, unspoken issues are quietly growing. Conflict itself is not the enemy; mishandled or ignored conflict is. Healthy conflict brings hidden tension into the light where it can be addressed and healed.

Avoiding conflict may keep you comfortable, but it keeps your culture stuck. Leaning into conflict with grace and truth creates clarity, resets expectations, and restores relationships. The goal is not to "win" an argument, but to win back unity and understanding. When leaders are brave enough to address issues early, they prevent bitterness from taking root.

Reflection Questions

1. What conflict have I been avoiding even though it needs attention?

2. How can I bring honesty and empathy together in hard conversations?

Author Quote — Coach David Angeron

"Conflict avoided turns into resentment — conflict resolved turns into strength."

MARCH 15 —
BE THE LEADER YOU NEEDED

"Carry each other's burdens." — Galatians 6:2

Every leader has walked through seasons where they wished someone had noticed, supported, guided, or believed in them more. Those experiences weren't wasted — they trained your heart. Now you have the opportunity to become for others what you once needed yourself. Leadership is not about reliving the pain; it's about redeeming it.

Think about the leader you needed:

- ♦ Wise but patient
- ♦ Firm but compassionate
- ♦ Honest but encouraging
- ♦ Present, not distant

Now reverse the roles. Somebody needs *you* to be that leader right now. Use your story, your scars, and your lessons as tools to lift others. When you lead with empathy and strength, people feel safe enough to grow and challenged enough to change. That's the kind of leader who shapes lives and legacies.

Reflection Questions

1. What leadership trait did I need most during difficult times?

2. How can I demonstrate that trait toward someone this week?

Author Quote — Coach David Angeron

"The leader you needed is the leader you are now called to become."

MARCH 16 —
HONOR IS THE GLUE OF UNITY

"Outdo one another in showing honor." — Romans 12:10

Unity doesn't just appear because people share a logo, a paycheck, or a mission statement. Unity is built when honor is normal, not rare. Honor is the decision to treat people as valuable, even when tensions rise, stress hits, or disagreements surface. It doesn't mean you always agree; it means you always respect.

Honor means:

♦ Speaking respectfully
♦ Recognizing effort
♦ Celebrating progress
♦ Addressing issues with dignity
♦ Valuing strengths rather than magnifying flaws

Dishonor slowly eats away at trust. Sarcasm, gossip, eye rolls, dismissive tones, and public embarrassment tear teams apart more than strategy ever can repair. Honor doesn't ignore problems — it faces them — but it does so without attacking identity or worth. In an honoring culture, people feel safe enough to be honest and humble enough to grow. Where honor is present, unity becomes strong enough to withstand pressure, change, and conflict.

Reflection Questions

1. How can I create a culture where honor is normal and expected?

2. Who can I publicly honor this week for effort, progress, or growth?

Author Quote — Coach David Angeron

"Honor builds unity — unity builds victory."

MARCH 17 —
SEEK WISE COUNSEL

"Plans fail for lack of counsel, but with many advisers they succeed."
— Proverbs 15:22

Leadership doesn't mean having all the answers — it means knowing where to get them. Pride whispers, "You should have this figured out alone." Humility says, "I don't know everything, and that's okay." Wise leaders surround themselves with people who can see what they might miss. Counsel is not a sign of weakness; it's a safeguard against blind spots and impulsive decisions.

Seek counsel from people who:

♦ Share your values
♦ Understand your vision
♦ Tell you the truth, not what you want to hear
♦ Have fruit in the area where you seek advice

Social media opinions are loud, but godly wisdom is steady. The voices you allow in your ear shape the choices you make with your life, your team, and your organization. The right voices help you avoid unnecessary pain and accelerate progress. The wrong voices flatter your ego and damage your future.

Reflection Questions

1. Do I seek wisdom — or do I only seek agreement?

2. Who are the voices I should be listening to more intentionally?

Author Quote — Coach David Angeron

"Leaders don't rise alone — they rise with wise voices behind them."

March 18 — Develop Leaders, Not Dependents

"Equip God's people for works of service." — Ephesians 4:12

The true test of leadership is not how things run when you're present — it's how they run when you're not. Insecure leaders build dependence: people have to ask them everything, wait for their approval, and rely on them to solve every problem. Secure leaders build leaders. They don't hoard authority — they share it. They don't fear strong people — they develop them.

Develop leaders by:

- ◆ Delegating real responsibility
- ◆ Providing coaching and feedback
- ◆ Letting people fail safely
- ◆ Celebrating growth, not just perfection

Yes, development takes time. Yes, delegation can feel risky. But if everything depends on you, the organization's capacity will always be capped at your limits. When you build leaders, you multiply impact. The highest compliment to your leadership is not, "We need you for everything," but, "Because of you, we can now lead too."

Reflection Questions

1. Am I empowering people to lead, or making them dependent on me?

2. Who can I stretch, develop, and challenge next?

Author Quote — Coach David Angeron

"Your greatness isn't measured by how many people you lead — but by how many leaders you build."

MARCH 19 — MOMENTUM THROUGH MOTIVATION

Motivation is not fluff — it's fuel. People can know what to do and even how to do it, but if they're discouraged, exhausted, or unseen, their effort will fade. Leadership is more than assigning tasks; it's about stirring hearts. Motivation doesn't mean pampering people or lowering standards — it means reminding them why the work matters and why *they* matter.

Motivated teams don't just show up — they show up engaged. Motivation grows when leaders communicate purpose, celebrate wins, acknowledge effort, and speak life when others are struggling. Sometimes a single conversation, text, or word of affirmation can reignite a fire that was close to going out. When leaders intentionally fuel motivation, culture becomes energized, and momentum starts to build almost naturally.

Reflection Questions

1. How can I increase motivation across my team this week?

2. Who needs to hear that they are valued and capable?

Author Quote — Coach David Angeron

"Motivation is not hype — it's fuel."

March 20 — Appreciation Creates Acceleration

"Encourage the disheartened." — 1 Thessalonians 5:14

Appreciation may seem small, but it has massive impact. People can work for a paycheck, a title, or a goal — but they stay and stretch for leaders who genuinely appreciate them. When appreciation is absent, effort eventually becomes mechanical. When appreciation is present, effort becomes personal.

Recognize:

♦ Initiative
♦ Improvement
♦ Effort
♦ Attitude
♦ Character — not just results

A simple "thank you," a specific compliment, or a public acknowledgment can reignite someone's passion. Appreciation doesn't mean ignoring areas that need improvement; it means you don't overlook the progress that's already happening. The more appreciation flows from the top, the more it spreads across the whole organization. Highly appreciated people tend to become highly invested people — and highly invested people accelerate the mission.

Reflection Questions

1. Who deserves a "thank you" today that I haven't said yet?

2. How can I build appreciation into the culture consistently, not occasionally?

(You can keep your existing quote here, or add one if you'd like — I'll leave it open since you didn't specify an author line.)

MARCH 21 — RESOLVE HARD FEELINGS, DON'T BURY THEM

What's buried isn't gone — it's just growing underground. Unresolved conflict, offense, miscommunication, and disappointment eventually surface as distance, sarcasm, disengagement, or quiet resistance. Teams can keep producing while hearts are hurting, but sooner or later, the damage shows up in trust and unity.

Healing requires humility. It means being willing to say, "We need to talk," or "I may have misunderstood," or "That hurt me," or "I'm sorry." Hard conversations are uncomfortable, but they are far less costly than broken relationships. Leadership means stepping toward what is awkward so the team doesn't have to carry emotional baggage into tomorrow. When leaders model reconciliation, they give everyone permission to choose healing over hiding.

Reflection Questions

1. What relationship in my organization needs reconciliation or clarity?
2. How can I approach healing with humility and empathy?

Author Quote — Coach David Angeron

"Problems you ignore today will demand your attention tomorrow at a higher cost."

MARCH 22 — CULTURE PROTECTORS VS. CULTURE POISON

"Do not be misled: 'Bad company corrupts good character.'"
— 1 Corinthians 15:33

Every team has people who either protect culture or poison it. Culture protectors speak life, guard unity, uphold standards, and live the values even when it's inconvenient. Culture poison spreads gossip, negativity, excuses, and division — often in subtle ways at first. Over time, their influence can undo what took years to build.

A culture is strengthened not only by who you add — but by who you refuse to keep. Ignoring toxic behavior doesn't make you gracious; it makes you negligent. Leadership is not hoping problems disappear — it is confronting them with truth and honor. Reward those who carry the culture well. Have clear, courageous conversations with those who don't. If they refuse to change, you must protect the many from the few.

Reflection Questions

1. Who consistently protects culture — and how can I honor them?

2. What toxic behavior has been tolerated for too long?

Author Quote — Coach David Angeron

"If you don't correct culture poison, it will eventually replace culture protectors."

March 23 — The Leader's Table

E very leader creates an environment — a "table" where people gather, share ideas, and do life and work together. That table might feel tense, fearful, and performance-obsessed, or it might feel focused, safe, and mission-driven. People don't just remember what they did under your leadership — they remember how it felt to be led by you.

The best teams feel like family without losing standards. There's warmth, laughter, and encouragement — but also clarity, accountability, and high expectations. People are not walking on eggshells, but they are not walking casually either. They are respected, challenged, and included. When the table you set as a leader feels like a place of belonging, people bring their best ideas, their full energy, and their real selves.

Reflection Questions

1. Does my leadership atmosphere feel safe and demanding — or fearful and tense?

2. What can I do to make people feel valued while still upholding high standards?

Author Quote — Coach David Angeron

"If you want people to give their best, build a table where they feel they belong."

March 24 — The Blessing of the Right Partners

No significant God-sized assignment is meant to be carried alone. God advances leaders through strategic partners — people whose gifts, insight, perspective, and faith complement yours. The right partners multiply what you can do, see what you can't see, and stand with you when resistance comes. The wrong partners drain energy, dilute vision, and distract from purpose.

Partnerships must be built on:

- ◆ Shared values
- ◆ Mutual accountability
- ◆ Complementary strengths
- ◆ Unified mission

Partnership is not just about chemistry — it's about calling. Just because someone is gifted doesn't mean they're assigned to your journey. Be prayerful and discerning. The right partner doesn't just help you win — they help you win in a way that honors God, protects character, and sustains the mission.

Reflection Questions

1. Who in my life aligns with my spirit, mission, values, and calling?
2. Who am I trying to partner with that God may not have assigned to me?

Author Quote — Coach David Angeron

"Partners don't just multiply results — they multiply strength, wisdom, and faith."

MARCH 25 — WHEN TEAM MEMBERS BECOME FAMILY

There's a difference between a group of coworkers and a true team — and there's an even deeper difference when a team starts to feel like family. "Family" doesn't mean everyone is perfect or always agrees. It means people are deeply committed to one another beyond convenience. Wins feel shared. Challenges feel personal. Failure doesn't lead to abandonment — it leads to support and accountability.

In that kind of environment, people show up for more than a job. They show up for each other. They stay late for each other. They fight through pressure together. Family-level teams are built intentionally — through shared experiences, honest conversations, sacrificial decisions, and consistent encouragement. When people feel like family, they don't just protect the culture — they *own* it.

Reflection Questions

1. What can I do to deepen genuine connection, not just collaboration, within my team?

2. Who can I intentionally encourage or support this week?

Author Quote — Coach David Angeron

"Teams compete together — families fight for each other."

MARCH 26 —
THE WEIGHT OF LEADERSHIP

"My grace is sufficient for you." — 2 Corinthians 12:9

Leadership is heavy because it cares. You feel the pressure of decisions, the burden of people's futures, the tension of limited resources, and the emotional weight of conflict and uncertainty. Some days the mental load is heavier than anything on your calendar. That weight is not a sign you're failing — it's a sign you're invested.

But leadership was never meant to be carried in your own strength. God did not call you to lead so you could collapse under the responsibility. He called you to lead while depending on His grace. His strength is made perfect in your weakness — not in your pretending. You don't have to be the unbreakable hero; you need to be the surrendered leader. Bring the weight to Him daily.

Reflection Questions

1. Where do I need to depend more on God and less on myself?

2. Who can I be vulnerable with instead of pretending I'm fine?

Author Quote — Coach David Angeron

"Leadership requires strength — but lasting leadership requires surrender."

MARCH 27 — WHEN TO LET PEOPLE GO

"Walk with the wise and become wise." — Proverbs 13:20

One of the hardest parts of leadership is knowing when someone's season with you is over. Not everyone who starts with you is called to finish with you. People change, priorities shift, and sometimes values drift. Holding onto the wrong person too long out of guilt, fear, or nostalgia can silently damage your culture, discourage your top performers, and slow the mission.

Letting someone go is not a failure of care — it's a function of stewardship. When someone repeatedly resists feedback, dismisses standards, or undermines unity, love for the team requires action. You can be compassionate and still be decisive. You can honor someone's dignity even as you transition them out. Releasing is hard — but keeping the wrong fit is costly to everyone.

Reflection Questions

1. Is there someone I'm holding onto out of guilt instead of wisdom?
2. Is my compassion enabling dysfunction?

Author Quote — Coach David Angeron

"You don't protect a person by destroying the culture — you protect everyone by defending it."

March 28 —
Grace Without Enabling

"Be merciful, just as your Father is merciful." — Luke 6:36

Grace is powerful — but misunderstood grace can quietly destroy standards. Grace is God's heart to forgive, restore, and give people another chance. Enabling, however, is allowing someone to repeat unhealthy behaviors without consequence. Great leaders know how to extend mercy without abandoning responsibility.

Grace says: "I believe you can do better."

Accountability says: "But this pattern cannot continue."

The goal is not to crush people with perfection, but to call them higher with love and truth. When you extend grace, you offer support, coaching, and a path forward — not a free pass. The person who truly values the mission will treat grace as fuel to grow, not a license to slack. Lead with both compassion and conviction.

Reflection Questions

1. Where have I been extending grace without requiring growth?

2. How can I communicate both compassion and accountability clearly?

Author Quote — Coach David Angeron

"Grace is not the removal of standards — it is the opportunity to rise to them."

March 29 — Leadership That Listens

Influential leaders don't just speak well — they listen deeply. Listening communicates humility, respect, and genuine interest. When people feel heard, they become more open, honest, and engaged. When people continually feel ignored, they eventually shut down or drift away.

Great leaders listen to:

♦ Feedback
♦ Emotion
♦ Concerns
♦ Ideas
♦ Hidden meaning behind the words

Listening doesn't mean agreeing with everything you hear — it means understanding before responding. It means asking clarifying questions, paying attention to body language, and being present instead of distracted. A listening leader makes better decisions because they are informed by reality, not just assumption. When you listen to people, you earn the right to lead them.

Reflection Questions

1. Do I listen to respond or listen to understand?

2. Who needs to feel heard by me this week?

Author Quote — Coach David Angeron

"When leaders listen to people, people listen to leaders."

MARCH 30 —
RESPECT MUST BE EARNED DAILY

"Do to others as you would have them do to you."
— Luke 6:31

Respect is not a trophy you win once and keep forever. It is a daily decision and a daily demonstration. Titles can demand obedience, but only character earns respect. People watch how you handle pressure, how you treat those with less power, how you admit mistakes, and how you live when no one is watching.

People respect leaders who:

♦ Keep their word
♦ Respect others
♦ Treat everyone fairly
♦ Make decisions with integrity
♦ Lead by example

You don't get to opt out of character on hard days and still expect full respect. Leadership isn't about forcing people to follow — it's about living in such a way that they *want* to. When respect rises, influence rises. When respect falls, authority becomes fragile, no matter the position.

Reflection Questions

1. Do my actions earn respect — or do I expect it because of my role?

2. What decision or behavior can strengthen my credibility this week?

Author Quote — Coach David Angeron

"Respect does not come from leadership — leadership comes from respect."

March 31 — Celebrate Progress, Not Just Perfection

"Do not despise these small beginnings." — Zechariah 4:10

Perfectionism kills momentum. When leaders only celebrate finished goals, teams learn to stay quiet about small wins and ongoing growth. But God often moves in "small beginnings" — quiet improvements, early steps, and unseen faithfulness. Progress is proof that people are moving, learning, and fighting forward — and that is worth celebrating.

When leaders celebrate progress:

♦ Morale increases
♦ Motivation increases
♦ Loyalty increases
♦ Momentum increases

Celebration doesn't ignore what's still unfinished; it reinforces what's already being done well. It tells people, "I see you. I see your effort. I see your growth." When you consistently recognize progress, you encourage people to keep going when the finish line still feels far away. Over time, those small celebrated steps become major victories.

Reflection Questions

1. Where has there been real progress I haven't acknowledged?

2. Who deserves to be celebrated for growth — even if the goal isn't reached yet?

Author Quote — Coach David Angeron

"If you wait for perfection to celebrate, momentum will die on the way."

APRIL

SPIRITUAL BATTLE IN THE MARKETPLACE

April 1 — The Marketplace Is a Mission Field

For many people, the closest they will ever come to a sermon is watching how a believer conducts business. Boardrooms, break rooms, sales calls, and Zoom meetings are all modern-day mission fields. God doesn't place you in the marketplace by accident — He positions you on purpose. Influence isn't just about revenue and reach; it's about reflection — how clearly your life reflects Christ.

You don't need a microphone or a platform to minister. Your honesty in negotiations, your patience with difficult clients, your integrity when no one is watching, and your compassion toward coworkers speak loudly about the God you serve. Excellence opens doors, but character opens hearts. When you handle conflict differently, handle success humbly, and handle pressure with peace, people will notice the difference — and many will become curious about the Source behind it.

Business isn't separate from ministry — it is a major part of it for many leaders. Wherever God sends you, you are sent as His representative.

Reflection Questions

1. How can I represent Christ more intentionally in my everyday leadership?

2. What is one practical way I can be a light in the workplace this week?

Author Quote — Coach David Angeron

"You don't need a pulpit to spread the gospel — just influence and integrity."

April 2 — Your Calling Comes With Resistance

"Put on the full armor of God, so that you can take your stand against the devil's schemes." — Ephesians 6:11

Spiritual warfare often intensifies when you step into spiritual assignment. The closer you move toward purpose, the more the enemy attacks. Not because you're failing — but because you're a threat. The enemy is not intimidated by casual, distracted believers; he is threatened by focused, obedient leaders who build the Kingdom through their business, influence, and decisions.

Resistance doesn't always mean you missed God. In many cases, resistance is evidence that you're exactly where you're supposed to be. That's why you must learn to fight the right way. You don't win spiritual battles with more hustle, more stress, or more control. You win them with prayer that covers your team, worship that centers your heart, Scripture that anchors your mind, and faith that refuses to quit.

Instead of asking, "Why is this so hard?" ask, "What is God building in me — and what is the enemy trying to stop?"

Reflection Questions

1. Where am I experiencing resistance that might actually confirm my calling?

2. What spiritual discipline do I need to strengthen to stand firm?

Author Quote — Coach David Angeron

"The enemy doesn't attack the insignificant — he attacks the influential."

APRIL 3 — GOD GOES BEFORE YOU

"The Lord himself goes before you and will be with you." — Deuteronomy 31:8

As a leader, it's easy to feel like you're stepping into unknown territory — new ventures, tough conversations, major decisions, or unfamiliar assignments. But spiritually, you are never the first one there. God goes ahead of you into boardrooms, negotiations, interviews, strategic meetings, and difficult seasons. He is already working in hearts, aligning timing, and arranging circumstances you can't see yet.

When you believe that God goes before you, fear turns into confidence. You stop living like everything depends solely on your preparation and begin walking like you are partnering with a God who is always ahead of you. That doesn't remove planning or responsibility — it removes panic. Your job is obedience; His job is orchestration.

You may not know how everything will play out, but you do know Who has already stepped into tomorrow. Courage grows when you realize each step of faith is not trailblazing alone — it's following a God who has gone first.

Reflection Questions

1. Where do I need to act with confidence because God has already gone before me?

2. What situation am I trying to control rather than trust God with?

Author Quote — Coach David Angeron

"You don't walk into unknown territory —
you walk into territory God already prepared."

April 4 — Fight the Right Battles

Not every conflict is your calling. The enemy loves to bait leaders into battles that drain emotional energy, destroy focus, and distract from assignment: petty arguments, online debates, ego-driven competition, old offenses, and endless attempts to prove yourself. You can win those arguments and still lose ground in your purpose.

Your God-given fight is for things that matter eternally:

- Faith — staying anchored in God's truth
- Family — protecting the relationships entrusted to you
- Calling — staying faithful to what God assigned
- Integrity — guarding your character when no one is watching
- Culture — building healthy environments
- People — fighting for those you lead and love

The enemy cannot defeat you if you stay in the battles God called you to, but he can wear you out in the ones God never assigned. Wisdom is knowing when to walk away and when to stand firm.

Reflection Questions

1. Have I been fighting battles that don't matter?

2. What mission-critical fight requires my attention instead?

Author Quote — Coach David Angeron

"The enemy cannot defeat you — but he can distract you into defeating yourself."

April 5 — Prayer Is a Leadership Strategy

"Pray without ceasing." — 1 Thessalonians 5:17

Prayer is not the last resort of desperate leaders — it is the first strategy of wise ones. In business and leadership, God cares about more than your private spiritual life; He cares about your decisions, your staff, your investors, your customers, and your direction. Prayer invites God's wisdom into board decisions, His timing into opportunities, His protection over your team, and His favor over your work.

Leaders pray for wisdom when choices are complex, discernment when motives are unclear, unity when opinions clash, and courage when fear whispers. Working hard is essential, but working without prayer is dangerous. You'll carry weight you weren't built to carry alone.

Work like it depends on you — but pray like it depends on God. Prayer doesn't slow execution; it clarifies execution. It saves you from wrong partnerships, wasted efforts, and premature moves.

Reflection Questions

1. Do I lead from prayer or only pray once problems appear?

2. What decision or challenge do I need to bring to God today?

Author Quote — Coach David Angeron

"The leader who prays will always outlast the leader who only performs."

April 6 — When God Removes People

"They went out from us, but they did not really belong to us." — 1 John 2:19

Some of the hardest moments in leadership are when people leave — staff, partners, friends, or key team members. It can feel like failure, betrayal, or loss. But sometimes, what feels like subtraction is actually God's protection. He sees attitudes, motives, and future decisions you cannot see yet. He knows when keeping someone connected to your assignment would damage what He's building.

Not every departure is a rejection of you — some are a redirection from God. Instead of clinging to who left, trust the One who remains. Release people gracefully. Bless them as they go. Refuse to become bitter, resentful, or suspicious of everyone else because of one painful exit.

God is faithful to send the right people in the right seasons. When He allows someone to leave, it's because the next chapter will require a different alignment.

Reflection Questions

1. Have I been trying to hold onto someone God already removed?

2. Do I trust God enough to allow change without bitterness?

Author Quote — Coach David Angeron

"Some relationships don't end because they failed — they end because they fulfilled their assignment."

April 7 — God Turns Attacks Into Advancement

"You intended to harm me, but God intended it for good." — Genesis 50:20

The enemy's attacks are real — betrayal, criticism, lies, unfair treatment, lost opportunities, or unexpected setbacks. But none of those things have the final word over a leader surrendered to God. What others meant to break you, God can use to build you. What was designed to slow you down, God can use to refine your character and sharpen your discernment.

Every attack carries an opportunity: to grow thicker skin but a softer heart, to learn who is truly for you, and to deepen your dependence on God instead of on status or approval. In God's hands, wounds become wisdom, and opposition becomes preparation.

You are not just surviving what hit you — you are being strengthened by it. When you look back, you will see that God used what was meant to harm you as a stepping stone into a stronger, wiser, more surrendered version of yourself.

Reflection Questions

1. What painful situation has God already started turning for good?
2. What did I gain (wisdom, resilience, clarity) from what was meant to hurt me?

Author Quote — Coach David Angeron

"What comes against you becomes fuel for what God is building within you."

April 8 — When You Don't Know What to Do

"If any of you lacks wisdom, let him ask of God." — James 1:5

Leadership guarantees you will face moments where the stakes are high and the answers are unclear. Data is helpful, experience is valuable, and counsel is important — but there are decisions where none of that feels like enough. That's when you don't need more information; you need wisdom.

God's wisdom is more than clever ideas — it is insight that sees around corners you can't see. He can give you clarity, conviction, and peace that doesn't make sense on paper but proves right over time. He speaks through His Word, through godly counsel, through a check or peace in your spirit, and through doors that open or close.

You don't have to pretend you always know what to do. You simply have to be humble enough to ask and patient enough to listen. Wisdom is available — but it must be sought.

Reflection Questions

1. Where am I leaning on my own understanding instead of asking for God's wisdom?

2. What decision requires prayer instead of pressure?

Author Quote — Coach David Angeron

"Every problem has a solution — and wisdom is the map to find it."

APRIL 9 — LEAD FROM THE SPIRIT, NOT THE STRESS

"Walk by the Spirit." — Galatians 5:16

Leadership comes with pressure — deadlines, expectations, financial weight, and people's needs. When stress is unfiltered, it often comes out as anger, impatience, harsh words, or rushed decisions. That's when the flesh starts leading instead of the Spirit.

But when you slow down and choose to be led by the Holy Spirit, everything shifts. You begin to see problems with God's perspective instead of panic. Stress becomes a signal to lean into God's presence, not a license to lose control. He can turn fear into courage, frustration into wisdom, and exhaustion into renewed dependence.

Leaders are most dangerous to the enemy when they operate from peace rather than pressure. The enemy will push you to hurry, react, and explode. The Spirit will lead you to pause, listen, and respond. One voice burns you out; the other builds you up.

Reflection Questions

1. Am I leading today from stress, emotion, or the Holy Spirit?

2. What practical step helps me shift from pressure to peace?

Author Quote — Coach David Angeron

"The enemy pushes — the Spirit leads. Follow the right voice."

APRIL 10 —

VICTORY BEGINS IN YOUR MIND

"Be transformed by the renewing of your mind."
— Romans 12:2

The mind is the frontline of spiritual warfare. Before defeat shows up in behavior, it grows in belief. Thoughts of "I'm not enough," "This will never change," "I'm failing," or "I'm alone" become heavy chains if they're left unchallenged. The enemy doesn't always need to change your circumstances — he just needs to convince you that your situation is hopeless.

Renewing your mind means replacing lies with truth. It means feeding on God's Word until what He says becomes louder than self-doubt, insecurity, anxiety, and comparison. Transformation doesn't come from one verse one time; it comes from a steady diet of truth day after day.

What you repeatedly meditate on will eventually show up in your decisions, your leadership, and your emotional health. If your thoughts change, your life will follow. Victory starts when you stop agreeing with defeat in your mind.

Reflection Questions

1. What thought pattern has been limiting my boldness, joy, or confidence?

2. What Scripture can I speak daily to renew my mindset?

Author Quote — Coach David Angeron

"The enemy attacks your mind because he fears your potential."

APRIL 11 — FAITH IS A WEAPON

Faith is not passive optimism — it's a defensive and offensive weapon. The enemy fires "arrows" of fear, doubt, accusation, and discouragement at leaders. If you absorb every thought and feeling as truth, those arrows wound deeply. Faith lifts the shield and says, "That's not what God said."

Faith doesn't pretend the challenges aren't real; it simply declares that God's promises are more real. When circumstances scream that you're alone, faith speaks, "God is with me." When fear whispers that you're unqualified, faith declares, "God called and equipped me." Faith refuses to let external pressure override internal conviction.

Fear reacts to circumstances; faith responds to calling. You can't always control what comes against you, but you can choose whether to raise the shield or drop it.

Reflection Questions

1. Where do I need to lift the shield of faith instead of surrendering to fear?

2. What promise from God do I need to stand on today?

Author Quote — Coach David Angeron

"Faith is not avoiding fear — it is attacking fear with truth."

APRIL 12 — WORSHIP WINS WARS

"The Lord is my strength and my song." — Exodus 15:2

Worship is more than singing at church — it is a powerful weapon in spiritual warfare. When pressure mounts, your mind fills with what-ifs, worst-case scenarios, and anxious thoughts. Worship interrupts that cycle and redirects your focus from the size of the problem to the greatness of God.

Worship starves worry and feeds faith. It reminds your soul, "God is still on the throne. He has not changed. He is still faithful." It shifts the atmosphere in your heart, your home, and even your workplace. When leaders choose to worship in the middle of stress, they model a different way of fighting battles.

Worship doesn't always change the situation immediately, but it changes you in the situation — strengthening, steadying, and centering you in God's presence. A worshiping leader becomes hard for the enemy to intimidate.

Reflection Questions

1. Do I worship only when life is peaceful — or especially when it isn't?

2. What worship habit can I add to my leadership routine?

Author Quote — Coach David Angeron

"Worship doesn't make battles disappear — it makes leaders undefeatable in them."

APRIL 13 —
DON'T NEGLECT YOUR ARMOR

"Put on the full armor of God." — Ephesians 6:11

No wise leader walks into a high-stakes meeting unprepared — yet many walk into spiritual battles uncovered. God has provided spiritual armor, but He will not force it onto you. You must choose to "put it on" daily, intentionally.

Armor includes:

♦ Truth — grounding yourself in God's Word, not opinions

♦ Righteousness — living with integrity and obedience

♦ Peace — standing firm in God's presence, not panic

♦ Faith — trusting God over what you see

♦ Salvation — remembering whose you are

♦ The Word of God — actively using Scripture as your weapon

Every day you lead without armor, you step into unseen warfare unprotected. But when you start your day aligning your mind, heart, and spirit with God, you become far harder to shake. The goal is not to avoid battles, but to be properly armed when they come.

Reflection Questions

1. Which part of the armor of God do I need to strengthen?

2. How can I create a routine to start each day spiritually protected?

Author Quote — Coach David Angeron

"The danger isn't in facing battles — it's in facing them unarmed."

APRIL 14 — GOD WILL VINDICATE YOU

"The Lord will fight for you; you need only to be still." — Exodus 14:14

Leadership sometimes means being misunderstood, misrepresented, or even lied about. Your instinct may be to argue, defend yourself, and correct every narrative. But there are moments when the most powerful act of faith is to stay obedient, stay upright, and let God handle your reputation.

God sees every private conversation and hidden motive. He knows the truth behind distorted stories. When you keep your heart clean and your hands steady, He has a way of revealing truth in His timing. Vindication may not always be immediate, but it will be accurate.

Your job is to walk in integrity, not to chase every opinion. People may talk for a season, but God's favor lasts longer than gossip. Let your character speak louder than any accusation, and trust God to speak when you stay still.

Reflection Questions

1. Where have I been trying to fight battles that God wants to handle?

2. What situation requires trust instead of retaliation?

Author Quote — Coach David Angeron

"You don't have to chase lies when God Himself reveals truth."

APRIL 15 — DON'T LET WEARINESS WIN

The enemy doesn't always try to stop you with one big blow; sometimes he slowly drains you through constant pressure, disappointment, and delay. Weariness whispers lies like, "This isn't working," "You're wasting your time," or "Nothing is changing." Yet often, God is moving most quietly right before the breakthrough becomes visible.

Doing good can be tiring — especially when results feel slow. But just because you don't see immediate fruit doesn't mean seeds aren't growing. Heaven's timeline rarely matches our expectations. The call is not to feel strong every day, but to stay faithful every day.

When your soul feels tired, don't just grind harder — reset deeper. Rest, pray, worship, seek wise counsel, and allow God to renew your strength. The harvest belongs to those who don't quit.

Reflection Questions

1. What area of my calling has felt heavy or discouraging lately?
2. What can I do this week to restore my spiritual and emotional strength?

Author Quote — Coach David Angeron

"The enemy attacks hardest when the breakthrough is closest."

APRIL 16 — STAND YOUR GROUND

"After you have done everything, to stand." — Ephesians 6:13

Some seasons of leadership are full of movement — new ideas, doors opening, changes happening fast. Other seasons are about endurance. You've prayed, prepared, obeyed, and pushed... and God's instruction is simple: *stand*. Standing is not passivity; it's spiritual stubbornness. It's saying, "I will not back off what God said, even when I don't see what God promised yet."

Stand when:

- ◆ Progress feels slow
- ◆ Pressure feels high
- ◆ Critics get loud
- ◆ You feel unqualified

Standing doesn't mean you stop growing or stop listening — it means you stop retreating. The enemy's goal is to wear you down until you voluntarily walk away from territory God already gave you. Standing is a declaration: *I may feel tired, but I am not turning back.* You hold the line in faith until God moves in power.

Reflection Questions

1. Is there an area of my calling where I need to stand instead of retreat?

2. What Scripture strengthens my resolve when I feel tempted to quit?

Author Quote — Coach David Angeron

"When you refuse to retreat, the enemy loses his strategy."

APRIL 17 — DON'T PANIC — PRAY

"In everything, by prayer and petition... present your requests to God."
— Philippians 4:6

Panic and prayer may be triggered by the same problem — but they produce completely different outcomes. Panic magnifies the problem, clouds your judgment, increases fear, and rushes you into decisions you later regret. Prayer magnifies God, clears your perspective, calms your emotions, and positions you to respond with wisdom.

The enemy wants leaders to react, not seek God. He wants you so overwhelmed that you forget Who is actually in control. God, on the other hand, invites you to trade anxiety for access — direct access to His peace, wisdom, and presence.

Before you send the email, pray. Before you walk into the meeting, pray. Before you confront the issue, pray. You will never regret a decision made from a place of prayerful peace. But choices made in panic often create more problems than they solve.

Reflection Questions

1. What situation has triggered panic instead of prayer?

2. What would change if I paused to pray before responding?

Author Quote — Coach David Angeron

"Panic rushes — prayer resets."

April 18 —

God Strengthens the Outnumbered

"If God is for us, who can be against us?" — Romans 8:31

Leadership will place you in rooms where your convictions are in the minority. You may be the only one standing for integrity, the only one voicing what's right, or the only one willing to say, "This doesn't honor God." In those moments, it can feel like you're outnumbered — but Heaven's math is different.

You and God are always the majority. His favor outweighs opposition. His power outweighs pressure. Throughout Scripture, God consistently used outnumbered people — Gideon's army, David against Goliath, Daniel in Babylon — to show that outcomes belong to Him, not to popular opinion.

If standing for righteousness leaves you standing alone, stand anyway. Compromise may make you more comfortable in the moment, but it weakens your calling over time. God does some of His greatest work when the odds look impossible, just to prove the outcome was never dependent on numbers.

Reflection Questions

1. Where have I been shrinking back because I feel outnumbered or underestimated?

2. How can I lead boldly even if I'm the only one holding the standard?

Author Quote — Coach David Angeron

"With God on your side, you're never outnumbered — you're outmatched."

April 19 — God Always Finishes What He Starts

Callings don't unfold in straight lines. There are seasons where progress is visible and exciting — and seasons where everything feels stalled, confusing, or silent. In those quieter stretches, the enemy whispers, "Maybe you missed it. Maybe God is done with you. Maybe this is where it ends." But God's Word says otherwise.

If God started it, He plans to finish it. He doesn't abandon assignments or half-build destinies. The timeline is His, the process is His, and the glory is His. Your responsibility is not to understand every twist and turn, but to stay faithful in every season — especially when feelings don't match your faith.

Don't measure progress only by visible results. Measure it by obedience, character, and consistency. God does some of His deepest work in hidden seasons. Trust that the Author of your calling is also the Finisher.

Reflection Questions

1. Where am I doubting a work God has already begun in me?
2. What step of obedience do I need to continue even without results yet?

Author Quote — Coach David Angeron

"If God started it, it cannot end in defeat — only in completion."

April 20 — The Enemy Attacks What Matters Most

"The thief comes only to steal and kill and destroy." — John 10:10

Spiritual attacks are specific, not random. The enemy doesn't waste energy on what doesn't matter — he goes after what is most valuable: your faith, your family, your mission, your peace, your integrity, and your key relationships. When you notice unusual pressure in those areas, you're not just dealing with "bad luck" — you may be facing a targeted attack.

If he can shake your faith, he can weaken your confidence. If he can disrupt your family, he can distract your focus. If he can drain your peace, he can cloud your decisions. Recognizing this changes how you respond. Instead of just getting frustrated, you get strategic. You begin to guard what matters with prayer, boundaries, accountability, and intentional rest.

Pressure on valuable areas is not proof that God has left you — it's proof that your calling matters. Guard what the enemy is clearly targeting.

Reflection Questions

1. What valuable area in my life is facing the greatest attack right now?

2. What defenses (prayer, boundaries, accountability) do I need to reinforce immediately?

Author Quote — Coach David Angeron

"The enemy doesn't attack what's worthless — he attacks what's powerful."

April 21 — Peace Is a Spiritual Advantage

"The peace of God... will guard your hearts and your minds." — Philippians 4:7

In a world addicted to urgency, anxious leaders feel normal. But anxious leaders are easier to manipulate, distract, and derail. Peace is not weakness; it's a weapon. It allows you to think clearly when others are clouded, to respond instead of react, and to hear God's voice above the noise.

The enemy wants you frantic, rushed, and emotionally scattered. God wants you grounded, focused, and steady. Peace doesn't mean the absence of pressure — it means the presence of God *in* the pressure. When you carry peace into chaotic rooms, you bring something supernatural into natural environments.

Peaceful leaders make better decisions, communicate more clearly, and inspire more trust. They are not led by headlines, emotions, or opinion swings — they are led by the Spirit. In business and in spiritual warfare, peace gives you an undeniable advantage.

Reflection Questions

1. Am I making decisions from peace or pressure?
2. What habit helps me return to peace most effectively?

Author Quote — Coach David Angeron

"Peace is not the absence of pressure — it's the presence of God in it."

April 22 — The Devil Uses Discouragement

Discouragement is one of hell's most subtle and effective weapons. It doesn't show up as a sudden explosion — it seeps in quietly. You start questioning whether your sacrifices matter, whether your prayers are working, whether the vision is realistic. Over time, effort slows, passion fades, and leaders settle into survival.

Discouragement doesn't mean you're failing; it often means you're pushing into territory the enemy doesn't want you to reach. He knows he can't revoke your calling — but if he can convince you to quit, he doesn't have to. That's why you must treat discouragement like an attack, not a personality trait.

Don't let temporary emotions create permanent decisions. Lean into what fuels your spirit — God's Word, worship, wise friends, mentors, testimonies, and reminders of God's past faithfulness. Your confidence has a reward attached to it. Don't throw it away.

Reflection Questions

1. What discouraging thought have I been partnering with instead of resisting?

2. Who or what encourages my spirit that I need to lean into this week?

Author Quote — Coach David Angeron

"Discouragement is the enemy's way of getting you to surrender progress that's already working."

121

APRIL 23 —

THE POWER OF YOUR WORDS

"Death and life are in the power of the tongue." — Proverbs 18:21

Your words are not neutral — they carry weight. As a leader, what you say can either agree with the enemy's lies or align with God's truth. You can speak defeat over yourself ("I'm not enough," "This will never work," "I always mess this up"), or you can speak life ("God called me," "I am growing," "He is with me").

Your mouth can either tear down your confidence or strengthen it. It can spread fear or build faith in your team. Words spoken in frustration can crush someone's spirit; words spoken in intentional encouragement can revive it. The spiritual atmosphere around you often follows the language within you.

If you want to see change in your culture, your home, or your leadership, start with your vocabulary. Speak what God says, not what fear suggests. Declare His promises over your assignment.

Reflection Questions

1. What negative statement do I need to stop speaking?

2. What truth do I need to declare over my life and leadership daily?

Author Quote — Coach David Angeron

*"The enemy wants to use your voice against you —
God wants to use it through you."*

April 24 — The Enemy Attacks Through Isolation

"Two are better than one." — Ecclesiastes 4:9

One of the enemy's quiet strategies is isolation. If he can't stop your calling, he'll try to separate you from the people who strengthen it. Isolation rarely starts as rebellion; it usually starts as exhaustion, disappointment, embarrassment, or feeling misunderstood. Slowly, you stop answering calls, stop sharing honestly, stop asking for help — and that's when the enemy's lies get louder.

When leaders withdraw, insecurities echo. Fears feel bigger. Problems feel impossible. You were never designed to carry leadership alone. Even Jesus chose a team, shared burdens, and invited people into His hardest moments.

Instead of retreating, reach out — to mentors, trusted friends, pastors, coaches, or peers who share your values. Community doesn't remove battles, but it strengthens you to fight them.

Reflection Questions

1. Have I been isolating emotionally, mentally, or spiritually?

2. Who can I reach out to for honesty, prayer, or encouragement?

Author Quote — Coach David Angeron

"Isolation weakens leaders — community protects them."

APRIL 25 — DON'T GIVE THE ENEMY YOUR ENERGY

"Resist the devil, and he will flee from you." — James 4:7

Your energy is limited — and valuable. The enemy knows he can't cancel your calling, so he tries to drain the strength you need to walk it out. He'll use pointless arguments, petty conflicts, rumors, and drama to keep you distracted and exhausted.

Not every battle deserves your response. Not every comment deserves your explanation. Not every critic deserves your meeting. Wisdom is knowing when to resist and engage — and when to resist by simply ignoring and moving forward. Sometimes the most spiritual thing you can say is nothing.

Where your energy goes, your influence grows. If you give your best energy to distractions, you'll have nothing left for destiny. Protect your focus with boundaries, discernment, and a clear sense of assignment.

Reflection Questions

1. What — or who — has been draining my energy without contributing to my purpose?

2. What boundary do I need to set this week?

Author Quote — Coach David Angeron

"The enemy can't stop your calling —
but he will try to drain the energy needed to walk in it."

April 26 — God Uses Pressure to Produce Power

"When I am weak, then I am strong." — 2 Corinthians 12:10

Pressure is uncomfortable — but it's often purposeful. It reveals where you've been relying on yourself instead of God. It exposes cracks in your character, systems, or priorities so they can be strengthened. It stretches your capacity to handle more in the future.

God isn't trying to punish you with pressure; He's preparing you through it. Leaders who avoid every hard season stay shallow. Leaders who walk *through* pressure with God come out wiser, sturdier, and more effective. What feels like breaking is often building.

Instead of just asking, "Why is this happening?" ask, "What is God forming in me through this?" You may be developing resilience, patience, humility, or dependence on God at a level you've never known before. Those are the qualities that carry big callings.

Reflection Questions

1. Instead of asking "Why me?", can I ask "What is God building in me?"

2. What strength can only be developed through this season?

Author Quote — Coach David Angeron

"Pressure doesn't destroy leaders — it develops them."

April 27 — Anointing Makes You a Target — and a Threat

"Do not touch my anointed ones." — Psalm 105:15

The anointing on your life — God's empowerment for your assignment — makes you a threat to darkness. That's why the enemy doesn't attack you casually. He knows that if you walk fully in what God has placed on you, people will be freed, systems will shift, and lives will change.

Anointing attracts warfare, but it also guarantees protection. God is jealous over His anointed ones. What comes against you may feel intense — criticism, spiritual attack, misunderstanding, pressure — but it cannot ultimately succeed. The same oil that draws fire also draws favor.

Don't interpret every attack as proof that you're weak; often it's proof that you're significant. Instead of shrinking back or apologizing for being chosen, lean into the anointing with humility and boldness. You are both targeted and shielded.

Reflection Questions

1. Where have I mistaken spiritual attack for personal weakness?

2. How does understanding the anointing change how I handle adversity?

Author Quote — Coach David Angeron

"The anointing on your life is why the enemy attacks — and why he cannot win."

April 28 — Your Identity Is Your Defense

"You are God's masterpiece." — Ephesians 2:10

Spiritual warfare often starts with identity. If the enemy can convince you that you are unworthy, incompetent, or disqualified, he doesn't have to attack your assignment directly — you'll sabotage it yourself. That's why he whispers lies about who you are: "You're not enough. You're too broken. You're a fraud."

Identity secured in Christ is a shield. You are not defined by:

- ◆ Results
- ◆ Approval
- ◆ Money
- ◆ Titles

You are defined by what God has spoken over you — chosen, loved, forgiven, equipped, called. That truth doesn't change when circumstances swing or opinions shift. The more confident you are in who you are in Christ, the harder it is for the enemy's lies to land.

When you know your identity, you stop negotiating your worth and start walking in your destiny.

Reflection Questions

1. What lie about my identity do I need to reject today?

2. What truth about who I am in Christ do I need to embrace?

Author Quote — Coach David Angeron

"The enemy attacks identity because identity activates destiny."

April 29 — God Never Wastes a Battle

Every battle you face becomes raw material in God's hands. He wastes nothing — not the sleepless nights, not the tears, not the betrayal, not the disappointment. What felt like a detour will often become the very testimony that strengthens others.

Some of your greatest leadership wisdom will come from what hurt the most. You'll recognize dangers earlier, see patterns more clearly, and lead with greater empathy because you've *been there*. The enemy intended those moments to break you; God intends to use them to build you — and to build others through you.

The very battles that tried to bury you become platforms for encouragement, teaching, and breakthrough for others. Your scars become signs of survival — and then tools of ministry.

Reflection Questions

1. What hard season in my life became preparation rather than destruction?

2. How can my testimony help develop, encourage, or strengthen others?

Author Quote — Coach David Angeron

"The battle that tried to break you is the battle God will use to build you."

APRIL 30 — GOD IS TRAINING YOUR HANDS FOR BATTLE

"He trains my hands for battle; my arms can bend a bow of bronze."
— Psalm 18:34

Y ou are not weak because the fight is hard — you are being trained because the calling is great. God allows you to face pressure, complex decisions, spiritual resistance, and leadership challenges not to destroy your confidence, but to develop your capacity.

He is training your hands for battle — teaching you how to pray with authority, lead with wisdom, discern spiritual attack, handle conflict, and stay steady under weight. The strength you're building now is for battles and breakthroughs you haven't seen yet.

Every challenge is a classroom. Every trial is training. Growth is happening even when comfort is not. One day you'll handle with grace what once would have crushed you — and you'll realize God has been training you all along.

Reflection Questions

1. What current battle is strengthening my leadership the most?

2. How is God shaping me through this season rather than allowing it to break me?

Author Quote — Coach David Angeron

"God doesn't send battles to destroy you — He sends them to develop you."

MAY

MONEY, STEWARDSHIP
& MULTIPLICATION

MAY 1 — GROWTH IS INTENTIONAL, NOT ACCIDENTAL

"Make every effort to add to your faith…" — 2 Peter 1:5

Growth is never random. You don't wake up transformed just because you *want* to be better. Desire may ignite the vision, but discipline drives the process. God calls us to "make every effort" — that means leaning into practices, habits, and decisions that intentionally move us forward. If you drift through your days, you won't drift into growth; you'll drift into stagnation.

Leaders don't just ask, "What do I want?"

They ask, "What am I willing to do daily to get there?"

That means scheduling growth, not hoping for it. Reading, training, mentoring, reflection, prayer, evaluation — these aren't extras; they are essentials. Growth is a decision long before it becomes a result. When you choose consistent effort over comfort, development is no longer accidental — it becomes inevitable.

You can't control everything, but you can control whether or not you show up intentionally.

Reflection Questions

1. What growth habit have I been avoiding or delaying?

2. What one change would create the biggest growth in the next 30 days?

Author Quote — Coach David Angeron

"Growth isn't a dream — it's a disciplined lifestyle."

MAY 2 — GOD GROWS LEADERS BEFORE HE GROWS PLATFORMS

"Humble yourselves under God's mighty hand, that he may lift you up in due time."
— 1 Peter 5:6

God is far more interested in the strength of your character than the size of your platform. Before He expands your influence, He fortifies your foundation. Promotion happens internally before it ever shows up externally. If God elevates you before you are grounded, the very platform you prayed for will become a weight you cannot carry.

Sometimes delay isn't punishment — it's protection. Closed doors, slow growth, and hidden seasons can feel discouraging, but they are often God's way of building patience, humility, resilience, and integrity. He knows the pressure that comes with visibility. He refuses to put you in a place where your character cannot sustain your calling.

Private growth always precedes public promotion. When God is working on your heart, mindset, and maturity behind the scenes, it's a clear sign that He plans to use you in ways you can't fully see yet.

Reflection Questions

1. What internal strength is God developing in me right now?

2. Where do I need maturity before I ask for expansion?

Author Quote — Coach David Angeron

"When God is building you privately, it means He plans to use you publicly."

MAY 3 — VISION REQUIRES PRECISION

"Write the vision; make it plain." — Habakkuk 2:2

Vision is powerful — but only if it's clear. A vague vision may sound inspiring, but it doesn't move people. Vague dreams create vague results. When vision becomes precise, it becomes practical. Clarity is what turns a wish into a roadmap.

Your team can't follow what they don't understand. Vision must be:

◆ Simple
◆ Strategic
◆ Repeatable
◆ Inspiring

If you can't say it simply, you can't lead it effectively. A clear vision tells people where you're going, why it matters, and how they can help. It gives direction during distraction and focus during chaos. A blurry vision leads to blurry execution — and blurry outcomes. But a precise vision allows everyone to align decisions, energy, and effort toward the same destination.

Write it. Refine it. Repeat it. Let vision become the filter for what you say yes and no to.

Reflection Questions

1. Is the vision for my life or organization clear enough to repeat in one sentence?

2. Who have I communicated the vision to recently?

Author Quote — Coach David Angeron

"A vague vision is just a dream — a clear vision becomes a destiny."

MAY 4 — DREAMS DEMAND DISCIPLINE

"The diligent prosper." — Proverbs 13:4

Everyone has dreams — few are willing to embrace the discipline required to fulfill them. It's not what you *desire* that determines success; it's what you're disciplined enough to *do* consistently, especially when motivation fades. Discipline is the bridge between desire and destiny. Without it, dreams slowly turn into regrets.

Discipline is not easy — that's what makes it valuable. Discipline requires the courage to choose:

♦ Long-term gain over short-term comfort
♦ Purpose over pleasure
♦ Consistency over excuses

You can't expect championship-level results with convenience-level effort. If you're not willing to pay the price, don't ask for the prize. The good news is that discipline compounds. The more you show up, the stronger your habits become, and the easier it is to keep going. Over time, disciplined days become transformed lives.

Reflection Questions

1. What discipline, if mastered, would change everything in this season?

2. Where have I been waiting for motivation instead of building a habit?

Author Quote — Coach David Angeron

"People don't fail from lack of desire — they fail from lack of discipline."

May 5 — Great Leaders Remain Teachable

"The wise listen and add to their learning." — Proverbs 1:5

Success becomes dangerous when it kills teachability. The moment a leader decides, "I already know enough," their leadership begins to decline. The world is changing, people are changing, and problems are changing — which means you must keep growing. Teachability is a marketplace advantage and a Kingdom mindset.

Teachable leaders:

♦ Ask questions
♦ Invite feedback
♦ Seek mentors
♦ Read widely
♦ Learn from mistakes

They are more interested in growth than in being right. Pride says, "I already know." Wisdom says, "There's always more to learn." Leaders who stop learning eventually lead from outdated thinking, recycled strategies, and blind spots they refuse to see. Over time, their impact shrinks.

Great leaders stay students. The higher they go, the more they lean into learning — from God, from people, from experience, and even from failure.

Reflection Questions

1. Do I seek learning — or do I assume I already know?

2. What skills must I intentionally grow to reach my next level of leadership?

Author Quote — Coach David Angeron

"Leaders don't lose because they fail — they lose because they stop learning."

MAY 6 — EXECUTION OVER EXCUSES

Ideas are important — but execution changes lives. Talking about vision doesn't move it forward. Planning, strategizing, and dreaming are valuable, but without action, they become sophisticated forms of procrastination. God blesses the work of your hands, not just the wishes of your heart.

Execution requires:

- ♦ Decisiveness — choosing a direction
- ♦ Consistency — showing up again and again
- ♦ Accountability — allowing others to hold you to the standard
- ♦ Courage — moving even when there are no guarantees

At some point you must stop saying "one day" and start saying "today." Take the call, send the email, launch the initiative, write the chapter, make the hire, have the hard conversation. Work the plan — and the plan will work. God can open doors, but you must be willing to walk through them.

Reflection Questions

1. What task or step have I been delaying that I need to complete this week?

2. How can I move from intention to execution today?

Author Quote — Coach David Angeron

"God can't multiply action you never take."

MAY 7 —
STEWARD THE SEASON YOU'RE IN

"There is a time for everything." — Ecclesiastes 3:1

Every season carries an assignment. Some seasons are heavy building seasons; others are quieter seasons of learning, healing, or transition. Growth stalls when leaders fight the season instead of stewarding it. You waste energy wishing you were in a different place instead of maximizing where you are.

If it's a season of growth — learn deeply.

If it's a season of opportunity — act boldly.

If it's a season of rest — recover intentionally.

If it's a season of stretching — endure faithfully.

You don't get to control the timing, but you do control your response. Each season prepares you for the next: what you learn now will be needed later. When you honor the season instead of resenting it, you extract its full value.

Reflection Questions

1. What season am I in right now — and am I fighting it or stewarding it?

2. What mindset shift will help me embrace this season with maturity?

Author Quote — Coach David Angeron

"You can't rush what God is developing — but you can waste it by resisting."

May 8 — Focus Creates Favor

You can't build something great while being distracted by everything. Focus is one of the most underrated forms of stewardship. When your attention is scattered, your progress is slow. When your attention is aligned, your progress accelerates. God often blesses what you're willing to consistently focus on.

When you focus your time, resources, attention, and energy, you send a clear signal: "This matters." That focus draws clarity, solutions, opportunities, and sometimes even unexpected support. But when you say yes to everything, you dilute impact everywhere.

Focus attracts favor — distraction repels it. Every unnecessary commitment, every time-waster, every unfiltered "yes" steals energy from what matters most. Tighten your focus, and you'll often see momentum begin to move.

Reflection Questions

1. What priority deserves my full focus right now?
2. What distraction must be eliminated immediately?

Author Quote — Coach David Angeron

"Your life follows your focus — choose wisely."

MAY 9 — GROWTH REQUIRES PRUNING

"Every branch that does bear fruit He prunes so that it will be even more fruitful."
— John 15:2

God doesn't only prune what's dead — He prunes what's successful. A tree is trimmed not because it's failing, but because it's capable of more. That means God may cut back areas of your life that are "working" to make room for what is *best*. Pruning is uncomfortable because it feels like loss, but in the Kingdom, pruning is preparation for multiplication.

Pruning may look like:

♦ Changing direction
♦ Ending commitments
♦ Letting go of relationships
♦ Shifting priorities

Sometimes the good thing you're clinging to is blocking the great thing God wants to bring. When He removes, it's not to punish you — it's to position you. Growth requires making peace with endings, trusting that God knows what branches need to go for your life to bear more fruit.

Reflection Questions

1. What good thing is now limiting my growth because I'm holding onto it too tightly?

2. Where is God asking me to release something to multiply something?

Author Quote — Coach David Angeron

"Pruning doesn't reduce leaders — it refines them."

MAY 10 — EXCELLENCE IS A STEWARDSHIP ISSUE

"Whatever you do, work at it with all your heart, as working for the Lord."
— Colossians 3:23

Excellence isn't about perfectionism or impressing people — it's about honoring God. When you believe your assignment comes from Him, every task becomes an opportunity to worship. Excellence is doing your very best with what you have, right where you are, regardless of who is watching.

Excellence builds credibility, expands influence, and attracts opportunity. People trust leaders who take their work seriously. Mediocrity communicates carelessness — and it closes doors God intended to open. Excellence says, "I am grateful for this calling, and I will treat it like a gift, not a burden."

Excellence is not just what you do; it's how you do it — with integrity, effort, detail, and a desire to reflect God well in the marketplace.

Reflection Questions

1. Where have I tolerated mediocrity instead of pursuing excellence?

2. What effort or standard can I raise today?

Author Quote — Coach David Angeron

"Excellence is worship — it is how leaders show gratitude for their calling."

May 11 — Personal Growth Before Organizational Growth

Organizations rarely outgrow their leaders. Vision, innovation, culture, and momentum all flow from the leader's heart and mind. If the leader stops growing, the organization eventually hits a ceiling — one that no strategy or marketing campaign can break.

You can only lead people to levels you've reached yourself. If you grow in wisdom, your decisions improve. If you grow in emotional health, your relationships improve. If you grow in spiritual depth, your discernment improves. As you grow, the ripple effect touches every area of your leadership.

The most powerful investment you can make in your business, ministry, or team is the investment you make in yourself — your character, skills, mindset, and spiritual life. When the leader expands, the environment around them is forced to expand too.

Reflection Questions

1. What personal limitation is currently limiting my leadership capacity?

2. What learning, coaching, or discipline must I prioritize next?

Author Quote — Coach David Angeron

"When the leader grows, everything around the leader grows."

MAY 12 — BE OBSESSED WITH IMPROVEMENT

"Make the most of every opportunity." — Ephesians 5:16

Average leaders repeat the same year of experience ten times and call it a decade. Great leaders refuse to settle. They don't just ask, "Is it working?" — they ask, "How can it work better?" Improvement is a mindset, not a moment.

Growth is accelerated when you become obsessed with refinement — of systems, habits, communication, culture, and strategy. That obsession doesn't come from insecurity; it comes from stewardship. You realize that what God has given you is too important to manage casually.

Improvement requires curiosity, humility, and honest evaluation. It means being willing to hear hard feedback and adjust. Comfort kills growth — obsession with improvement multiplies it. Every day becomes an opportunity to do something just a little bit better than yesterday.

Reflection Questions

1. What system, habit, or strategy needs improvement?

2. Who on my team can help identify blind spots and opportunities?

Author Quote — Coach David Angeron

"You don't become world-class by being satisfied — you become world-class by being committed."

May 13 — Consistency Is a Leadership Superpower

"Let us not grow weary in doing good." — Galatians 6:9

Consistency separates starters from finishers. Many people have bursts of motivation; few have the discipline to keep showing up when the excitement fades. Talent may open doors, but consistency is what keeps them open.

Consistency means:

♦ Doing the right thing daily
♦ Showing up when you don't feel like it
♦ Holding standards even when no one is watching

Consistency compounds. Small, repeated actions — in health, leadership, relationships, finances, or spiritual life — create massive change over time. You don't always see the results immediately, but every day of faithfulness adds to the foundation.

The enemy wants to wear you out so you'll quit before the harvest. God calls you to keep sowing, trusting that due season always arrives for those who don't give up.

Reflection Questions

1. What area of my life lacks consistency the most?
2. What small daily habit will create major change over time?

Author Quote — Coach David Angeron

"Consistency doesn't make you perfect — it makes you unstoppable."

MAY 14 — LEADERS DON'T WAIT — THEY INITIATE

"Be strong and courageous." — Joshua 1:9

Indecision is one of the most subtle enemies of progress. Leaders who constantly delay, overthink, or wait for perfect conditions slowly lose influence and momentum. Courageous leaders don't have all the answers — but they move anyway, trusting God to guide mid-stride.

Most failure doesn't come from making the wrong decision; it comes from making no decision. Initiative is what separates leaders from spectators. It turns "someday" into "today." When you step out, even with some uncertainty, you create movement — and movement creates clarity.

You don't wait to feel ready; you decide to be ready. God often reveals the next step *after* you move, not before.

Reflection Questions

1. What decision have I been delaying due to fear or uncertainty?
2. What bold step can I take right now that moves the mission forward?

Author Quote — Coach David Angeron

"Leaders don't wait to feel ready — they decide to be ready."

MAY 15 — REMOVE WHAT WEAKENS YOU

"Throw off everything that hinders." — Hebrews 12:1

You can't run at full speed while carrying unnecessary weight. Growth requires subtraction as much as addition. Sometimes the greatest breakthrough doesn't come from adding something new — but from removing what's been slowing you down.

Eliminate:

♦ Toxic relationships
♦ Unhealthy habits
♦ Unproductive commitments
♦ Emotional baggage
♦ Excuses

You cannot become who you were designed to be while clinging to what was never meant to stay. Some things are not "sinful," but they are *heavy* — and heaviness hinders you. Wisdom is asking, "Does this strengthen me or weaken me? Does this move me forward or hold me back?"

Freedom creates fuel. When you let go of what drains you, you make room for what builds you.

Reflection Questions

1. What in my life is slowing me down instead of strengthening me?

2. What boundary or change needs to be made immediately?

Author Quote — Coach David Angeron

"Growth requires letting go — freedom creates fuel."

MAY 16 — GROWTH REQUIRES ACCOUNTABILITY

Accountability is not about control — it's about protection and sharpening. You will never reach your highest potential in isolation. Left alone, even strong leaders drift, compromise, soften, and slip into comfort. Accountability is God's way of surrounding you with people who refuse to let you settle for less than what He's placed in you.

You need people who will:

♦ Challenge you when you get comfortable
♦ Correct you when you drift off course
♦ Encourage you when you feel depleted
♦ Pray for you when you feel attacked
♦ Refuse to let you live beneath your calling

Accountability is uncomfortable because it confronts your blind spots — but that's exactly why it accelerates growth. Great leaders do not fear accountability; they *crave* it. They welcome hard conversations, honest feedback, and loving correction because they care more about destiny than ego.

If no one can challenge you, no one can sharpen you.

Reflection Questions

1. Who in my life can tell me the truth even when it's uncomfortable?

2. Where has avoiding accountability slowed my growth?

Author Quote — Coach David Angeron

"Accountability may sting for a moment — but stagnation lasts forever."

MAY 17 — GROWTH REQUIRES COURAGE

"Be strong and take heart, all you who hope in the Lord." — Psalm 31:24

Every new level of growth requires a new level of courage. You cannot step into a bigger future with a mindset built for survival. Growth will push you out of what's familiar into what feels risky — new rooms, new responsibilities, new standards, and new levels of spiritual warfare. Comfort is attractive, but it is also a cage. It keeps you safe from failure and also safe from purpose.

The life you want is on the other side of fear. The leader you are becoming lives beyond the walls of comfort. Courage doesn't mean you don't feel afraid; it means you move anyway, trusting that God is bigger than the risk. If the next step scares you, that's often a sign it matters. Fear screams, "What if you fall?" Faith whispers, "What if you fly?"

Don't wait for fear to disappear — choose courage in spite of it.

Reflection Questions

1. What opportunity am I avoiding because fear is louder than faith?

2. What bold act of courage would unlock the future I desire?

Author Quote — Coach David Angeron

"Growth begins where comfort ends."

MAY 18 — VISION WITHOUT STRATEGY IS JUST IMAGINATION

Vision is the picture of where you're going — but strategy is how you actually get there. Many leaders are overflowing with ideas yet frustrated with results. The gap is not passion; it's planning. God gives vision, but He expects leaders to build strategy. Prayer reveals the destination; wisdom designs the pathway.

Strategy creates:

♦ Priorities — what matters most right now
♦ Order — what must come first, second, and third
♦ Structure — how responsibilities and resources are organized
♦ Clarity — who is doing what and by when

Without strategy, vision remains a speech, not a reality. It stays on whiteboards and in notebooks instead of living in systems and actions. With strategy, vision becomes execution — decisions, tasks, timelines, and accountability. Don't just get excited about where you're going. Build a clear, measurable, step-by-step plan that brings the vision down to earth.

Reflection Questions

1. Do I have a plan — or just a desire?

2. What step-by-step structure can I implement to make the vision real?

Author Quote — Coach David Angeron

"Vision inspires — strategy delivers."

MAY 19 — PURPOSE MAKES PAIN PRODUCTIVE

"Our present sufferings are not worth comparing with the glory that will be revealed."
— Romans 8:18

Pain is inevitable — but misery is optional. The difference is purpose. Pain without purpose leads to bitterness, resentment, and quitting. Pain with purpose, however, becomes fuel for growth. God does not waste difficult seasons. He uses disappointment, delay, pressure, and even heartbreak to refine your focus, deepen your dependence on Him, and increase your capacity.

Growth hurts — but staying the same hurts too. When you understand that God is using the pressure to prepare you, pain becomes preparation, not punishment. Muscles are built through resistance; so are leaders. You begin to see trials not as proof that God has abandoned you, but as proof that He is developing you.

Everything you're facing is contributing to the leader you're becoming. One day, you will stand in a place you once prayed for, and you'll realize the pain was part of the process.

Reflection Questions

1. What difficult situation is refining me rather than ruining me?

2. What strength have I gained from past pain?

Author Quote — Coach David Angeron

"Pain is not a sign that you're breaking — it's a sign that you're building."

MAY 20 — VISION REQUIRES SACRIFICE

"To whom much is given, much will be required." — Luke 12:48

Y ou cannot live a common life and expect uncommon results. Every meaningful vision has a price tag. The clearer and higher the vision, the more sacrifice it demands — of time, comfort, habits, and sometimes even relationships that no longer align with your calling.

Success demands giving up:

- ◆ Laziness — choosing discipline instead
- ◆ Excuses — owning responsibility
- ◆ Distractions — protecting focus
- ◆ Familiarity — stepping into new environments
- ◆ Comfort — embracing growth and pressure

If you're not willing to sacrifice for the vision, the vision will eventually become the sacrifice. You'll either give up what holds you back, or you'll give up what God called you to build. Sacrifice is not loss — it is investment. What you lay down now makes room for what God wants to raise up later.

Reflection Questions

1. What am I holding onto that is slowing down the realization of the vision?

2. What sacrifice do I need to make to honor the calling on my life?

Author Quote — Coach David Angeron

"The vision won't grow until you grow — and growth always requires sacrifice."

MAY 21 — THE POWER OF CONSISTENT PLANNING

"Commit to the Lord whatever you do, and He will establish your plans."
— Proverbs 16:3

Planning doesn't guarantee success — but neglecting to plan almost guarantees chaos. When a leader's days are reactive instead of intentional, pressure becomes the driver. Planning is how you align time with purpose. It takes what matters most and gives it a place on your calendar, not just in your imagination.

Planning demonstrates:

- ◆ Intention — you know what matters
- ◆ Focus — you know what comes first
- ◆ Order — you reduce chaos and confusion
- ◆ Discipline — you're willing to structure your life for your calling

A leader without a plan is led by emergencies, interruptions, and emotions. A leader with a plan is guided by mission and priorities. Planning is not unspiritual; it's stewardship. You commit your plans to the Lord, then work them with diligence, inviting Him to direct, adjust, and bless.

Reflection Questions

1. Do I run my days — or do my days run me?

2. What planning habits do I need to implement weekly?

Author Quote — Coach David Angeron

"The future belongs to those who plan for it on purpose."

MAY 22 — PROTECT YOUR ENERGY LIKE YOUR CALLING DEPENDS ON IT

"Above all else, guard your heart." — Proverbs 4:23

Your energy is not unlimited — and it's not random. It is a God-given resource that fuels your calling. If you constantly give your best energy to drama, distractions, conflict, or people who drain you, you'll have nothing left for the assignment God placed on your life.

Energy drains come from:

- ◆ Drama and unnecessary conflict
- ◆ Distractions disguised as opportunities
- ◆ Overcommitment and poor boundaries
- ◆ Negativity and complaining environments
- ◆ Misaligned relationships and partnerships

Guarding your heart means guarding what affects your emotional, mental, and spiritual energy. Pay attention to what leaves you exhausted and what leaves you energized. Then align your schedule and boundaries accordingly. Protecting your energy is not selfish — it's strategic stewardship of your calling.

Reflection Questions

1. What consistently drains my energy?

2. What consistently restores it — and how can I prioritize that more?

Author Quote — Coach David Angeron

"Your calling can't operate at full strength if your energy is constantly depleted."

May 23 — Your Environment Shapes Your Excellence

"Walk with the wise and become wise." — Proverbs 13:20

You cannot live in an environment that fights your values and expect to thrive in your calling. Excellence grows where excellence is normal. If you stay in circles where mediocrity is accepted, excuses are celebrated, and gossip is constant, your standards will eventually slip.

Excellence is contagious — and so is mediocrity.

If you surround yourself with:

♦ Ambition and growth — you will be stretched
♦ Accountability and honesty — you will be sharpened
♦ Faith and vision — you will be encouraged

But if you surround yourself with complacency, excuses, and negativity, you will slowly shrink to fit the room.

Sometimes the most spiritual move you can make is to upgrade your environment — the people you spend time with, the culture you work in, and the voices you listen to daily. Change your environment, and your future begins to change with it.

Reflection Questions

1. Who around me makes me better — and who subtly weakens my drive?

2. Do my environments match the level of success I'm building?

Author Quote — Coach David Angeron

"Excellence isn't a personality trait — it's an environment."

May 24 — Momentum Comes From Mastery

"Do you see someone skilled in their work? They will stand before kings."
— Proverbs 22:29

Momentum isn't magic — it's the result of mastery. When you become excellent at what you do, you no longer have to chase opportunities; opportunities begin to find you. Doors open because your reputation walked into rooms before you did.

Mastery requires:

♦ Humility to admit you're not there yet
♦ Patience to practice long after the excitement fades
♦ Discipline to refine the small details others ignore
♦ Perseverance through frustration, repetition, and failure

Don't aim to be average at many things. Aim to be world-class at the thing God called you to do. The more you master your craft — in leadership, business, communication, coaching, or ministry — the more effective your impact becomes.

People may not see the hours of unseen work, but God does. Mastery honors Him and multiplies your influence.

Reflection Questions

1. What gift, skill, or calling do I need to master — not just maintain?

2. What practice or training could accelerate my mastery?

Author Quote — Coach David Angeron

"Mastery turns passion into purpose — and purpose into impact."

MAY 25 — GROWTH REQUIRES RISK

You cannot grow while clinging to complete safety. If you wait until all fear disappears and every variable is guaranteed, you will never move. Growth requires calculated risk — not recklessness, but Spirit-led, wisdom-informed courage.

Risk is stepping when you don't see the entire staircase, but you know Who asked you to move. It may look like launching the new project, having the hard conversation, hiring the person, changing direction, or stepping into a room where you feel out of your league.

Leaders who refuse risk remain in the small circle of what they already know. Leaders who embrace risk step into the future God designed for them. You can stay safe, or you can grow — but you cannot do both at the same time.

Reflection Questions

1. What calculated risk am I avoiding that could lead to growth?

2. What step of faith is God asking me to take?

Author Quote — Coach David Angeron

"Growth isn't just faith in God — it's the courage to act like He's backing you."

MAY 26 —
THE MYTH OF OVERNIGHT SUCCESS

Overnight success is a myth we see on social media, not in real life. What looks sudden to the world took years of unseen work — early mornings, late nights, quiet sacrifices, and private battles. Success is never sudden; *visibility* is.

Breakthrough happens when leaders:

♦ Stay consistent long after emotions fade
♦ Stay prepared even when doors seem closed
♦ Stay humble when no one is clapping
♦ Stay teachable through correction and failure

The world often only sees the "moment" — the launch, the promotion, the award, the milestone. God sees the process — the obedience, perseverance, faith, and integrity. Real success is built in the shadows long before it's celebrated in the spotlight.

Don't chase instant results. Chase long-term faithfulness.

Reflection Questions

1. Am I chasing sudden success or steady growth?
2. What long-term habit requires patience instead of pressure?

Author Quote — Coach David Angeron

"Success is never sudden — only recognition is."

MAY 27 — GREAT LEADERS WIN THE MORNING

"In the morning, Lord, you hear my voice." — Psalm 5:3

Mornings are not just about time — they're about trajectory. How you start your day shapes how you handle pressure, conflict, temptation, and opportunity. Great leaders don't roll into their day unprepared; they *set* their day with intention.

A winning morning includes:

- Prayer or quiet time — aligning with God's presence
- Planning — clarifying priorities and key tasks
- Movement or fitness — energizing your body
- Gratitude — shifting your mindset from scarcity to abundance
- Focus — deciding what will get your best attention

When you own your morning, you stop living in constant reaction mode. Chaos attacks leaders who haven't prepared mentally, spiritually, and strategically. You may not be able to control everything that happens, but you can control how you start.

Reflection Questions

1. Does my morning strengthen my leadership or weaken it?

2. What habit can I add tomorrow morning to elevate my mindset?

Author Quote — Coach David Angeron

"Control the morning — and you control the momentum."

MAY 28 — DON'T APOLOGIZE FOR HIGH STANDARDS

High standards are not arrogance — they are stewardship. If God has entrusted you with a calling, a team, a platform, or a business, it deserves your best. High standards protect the mission, shape the culture, and filter the people who genuinely belong with you.

Low standards create comfort.

High standards create champions.

Not everyone will like your standards. Some will accuse you of being too intense, too serious, or too demanding — but often that's because your standards expose their complacency. You're not responsible to make everyone comfortable; you're responsible to honor what God has placed in your hands.

Don't lower your standards to keep people. The right people will rise to them.

Reflection Questions

1. Have I lowered my standards to avoid conflict or disappointment?
2. Which standard needs to be reinforced immediately?

Author Quote — Coach David Angeron

"High standards don't push good people away — they push the wrong people away."

MAY 29 — HUNGER BEATS TALENT

Talent gets attention — hunger gets transformation. Talent may open the door, but hunger is what keeps you growing once you're inside. A talented person who lacks hunger becomes stagnant. A hungry person with average talent becomes dangerous because they refuse to stop improving.

Hungry leaders:

♦ Keep learning when others plateau
♦ Keep adapting when others resist change
♦ Keep improving when others feel "good enough"
♦ Keep showing up when others get bored

God blesses hunger — especially a hunger for Him and His ways. When you are hungry to grow, to honor Him, to maximize what He gave you, you become a candidate for greater responsibility.

Ask yourself: am I truly hungry, or am I coasting on past ability?

Reflection Questions

1. Am I driven by hunger — or coasting on ability?

2. What does an increased level of hunger look like in my leadership right now?

Author Quote — Coach David Angeron

"Talent opens doors — hunger walks through them."

MAY 30 —
SUCCESS REQUIRES SELECTIVE FOCUS

"No one can serve two masters." — Matthew 6:24

You can do many things, but you cannot master many things at once. Success is not just about addition — it's about subtraction and selection. The more divided your focus, the weaker your impact. If everything is a priority, nothing truly is.

Selective focus means having the courage to say:

- ♦ "Not now" to timing that isn't right
- ♦ "Not yet" to opportunities that don't align
- ♦ "Not my assignment" to good things that aren't *your* thing

You grow most when you give your best energy to the one or few things that matter most in this season. That's where excellence, momentum, and breakthrough live. Spreading yourself thin may feel productive, but it rarely produces mastery or lasting impact.

Reflection Questions

1. What good thing is stealing time from the most important thing?
2. If I could only focus on one goal for the next 90 days, what would it be?

Author Quote — Coach David Angeron

"You can do anything — but not everything. Focus is the secret advantage."

MAY 31 — PREPARATION UNLOCKS OPPORTUNITY

"The wise store up knowledge." — Proverbs 10:14

Most people pray for opportunities they are not prepared to handle. God is not just interested in opening doors — He's interested in what you'll do once you walk through them. Preparation is how you honor future favor before it arrives.

When you prepare faithfully, opportunities often appear "suddenly" — but they are never random. Favor rises to meet preparation. The door doesn't open because you wished for it; it opens because God sees a steward He can trust on the other side.

Prepare your skills. Prepare your systems. Prepare your mindset. Prepare your team. Develop now what the next level will demand later. When the opportunity comes, it will be too late to start preparing — but never too late to begin today for what's ahead.

Reflection Questions

1. What opportunity am I praying for that I need to prepare for more thoroughly?

2. What skill, system, or structure needs to be strengthened before the next level?

Author Quote — Coach David Angeron

"The future doesn't belong to the lucky — it belongs to the prepared."

✝

JUNE

COURAGE, PRESSURE & PERSEVERANCE

June 1 — Honor God With Your Finances

"Honor the Lord with your wealth." — Proverbs 3:9

Money isn't evil — but the love of money is. Finances are not neutral in leadership; they reveal who sits on the throne of your heart. When money becomes your master, anxiety, greed, and fear take over. But when money becomes a tool surrendered to God, peace replaces pressure.

Honoring God with your finances means inviting Him into *every* decision — tithing, generosity, saving, investing, spending, and even how you price your work. It means refusing to cut corners, manipulate, or operate in darkness. When your financial life becomes worship instead of worry, you begin to experience freedom. You stop chasing money and start stewarding it.

God doesn't just want to provide *for* you — He wants to teach you how to manage what He provides. Financial peace doesn't begin with more income; it begins with more obedience.

Reflection Questions

1. Are my financial decisions based on fear or faith?
2. What step can I take today to honor God with my finances?

Author Quote — Coach David Angeron

"Money is a tool — not a master. Steward it, don't serve it."

June 2 — Prosperity Has Purpose

God doesn't bless leaders just so they can live comfortable — He blesses them so they can live *impactful*. Prosperity in the Kingdom is not about flexing status; it's about increasing capacity. The more resources you have, the more ministries you can fund, families you can support, opportunities you can create, and kingdom work you can accelerate.

Prosperity is not selfish when generosity is your motive. God looks for people who won't hoard what He gives, but will channel it. When your heart says, "Lord, if You can get it *through* me, You can trust it *to* me," you become a candidate for increase.

This doesn't mean everyone will be a millionaire — but it does mean God desires you to live resourced, not restricted, so you can move when He says move and give when He says give. Prosperity is about assignment, not ego.

Reflection Questions

1. If God increased my resources tomorrow, how would I use them for kingdom impact?

2. Am I preparing for abundance or only surviving lack?

Author Quote — Coach David Angeron

"Prosperity has purpose — increase is a calling, not just a comfort."

JUNE 3 — GOD BLESSES WHAT YOU BUILD WITH WISDOM

"By wisdom a house is built." — Proverbs 24:3

Prayer can open doors — but wisdom determines whether what's behind those doors stands or falls. Many people can receive success; far fewer can sustain it. God may bless you with opportunity, but it is wisdom that creates order, structure, and protection around what He gives.

Wisdom doesn't come from emotion. It comes from:

♦ Scripture that shapes your decisions
♦ Godly counsel that challenges your blind spots
♦ Planning that anticipates problems before they arrive
♦ Humility that admits, "I don't know everything"

Impulse builds quickly and collapses just as fast. Wisdom builds slowly, steadily, and securely. God is not interested in just giving you a moment of blessing — He wants you to build something that outlives you. If you want success to last, build with wisdom, not reaction.

Reflection Questions

1. What area of my life needs more wisdom and less emotion?

2. Who can I learn from to become a wiser steward?

Author Quote — Coach David Angeron

"Prayer may open the door — but wisdom keeps it open."

JUNE 4 — HARD WORK HONORS GOD

"All hard work brings a profit." — Proverbs 14:23

God doesn't reward laziness. He blesses diligence, focus, and stewardship. Hard work isn't a curse — it's a calling. You've been given gifts, opportunities, and assignments that require effort to fully unlock. When you show up prepared, focused, and willing to give your best, you are honoring the One who trusted you with the task.

Hard work is not about hustling for your worth — your worth is settled in Christ. Hard work is about stewarding your calling. It's using your time wisely, being excellent in the details, and refusing to settle for halfway effort. When you see your work as worship, excellence becomes natural, not forced.

There is a difference between busyness and hard work. Busyness is scattered, frantic, and unfocused. Hard work is targeted, intentional, and aligned with purpose.

Reflection Questions

1. Am I working hard — or hoping for results without effort?
2. What area of my work ethic can be strengthened this week?

Author Quote — Coach David Angeron

"When you see your work as worship, excellence becomes natural."

June 5 — Wealth Without Wisdom Destroys

Money is not always a blessing — especially when it arrives in the hands of someone not ready to manage it. Wealth doesn't change character; it reveals and amplifies it. If there is discipline inside you, money multiplies impact. If there is chaos, pride, or impulsiveness inside you, money multiplies damage.

This is why God often develops wisdom before delivering wealth. He's not withholding from you out of cruelty; He's protecting you from destruction. He knows that unrestrained access to resources without maturity can lead to bondage — debt, addiction, arrogance, or poor stewardship.

Instead of only praying, "God, increase my finances," also pray, "God, increase my wisdom." Ask Him to form the habits, mindset, and character needed to carry more without collapsing under it.

Reflection Questions

1. Am I praying for blessing without seeking the wisdom to handle it?

2. What financial habits need to change before increase arrives?

Author Quote — Coach David Angeron

"Financial increase without character becomes financial injury."

June 6 — Increase Comes Through Faithfulness

God isn't impressed by big talk or big vision if there is no faithfulness in the small things. He promotes *faithfulness*, not just ambition. Before God multiplies anything in your life — money, influence, opportunity — He watches how you steward what you already have.

Are you excellent with the "little"? Do you handle small budgets with integrity? Do you prepare for small meetings like big ones? Do you treat small platforms with honor? Increase begins with gratitude and responsibility in your current season.

Many people are waiting for "more" before they get serious — more money, more followers, more recognition. But God's pattern is the opposite: be faithful now, and more will follow if it aligns with His will.

Reflection Questions

1. Am I faithfully managing what I already have, or waiting for more to start?

2. Where can I demonstrate excellence right now instead of later?

Author Quote — Coach David Angeron

"Faithfulness today invites favor tomorrow."

June 7 — You Can't Reap From Seeds You Never Plant

"A person reaps what they sow." — Galatians 6:7

G od's kingdom operates on a seed principle. Harvest is never random — it's always connected to what was planted. Many people crave results they've never actually sown for: strong relationships without time invested, financial stability without discipline, spiritual depth without prayer, business success without consistent work.

You cannot pray for what you refuse to plant. God will bless what you build — but He won't build what you refuse to start. Seeds can be time, money, ideas, encouragement, service, or sacrifice. Small, faithful seeds over time lead to large, impactful harvests.

If you don't like the harvest you're seeing, it's time to examine the seeds you're sowing — or not sowing.

Reflection Questions

1. What area of my life requires more intentional seed-sowing?

2. Am I expecting a harvest where I have not consistently invested?

Author Quote — Coach David Angeron

"You cannot expect results from places you refuse to invest."

June 8 — Your Budget Reflects Your Beliefs

"For where your treasure is, there your heart will be also." — Matthew 6:21

A budget is not restriction — it is direction. It is one of the clearest mirrors of your values. We can say we care about generosity, growth, and stewardship, but our spending reveals the truth. If you show me where your money goes, I'll see what your heart truly prioritizes.

Financial stewardship is spiritual maturity. It takes planning so your money has an assignment, not just an impulse. It takes discipline to say "no" in the moment so you can say "yes" to a bigger future. It takes restraint to live below your means and generosity to live beyond yourself.

Money follows belief — not emotion. When you truly believe God has called you to something great, your financial decisions begin to line up with that future.

Reflection Questions

1. Does my spending reflect my values — or my impulses?
2. What practical financial habit can I improve this month?

Author Quote — Coach David Angeron

"Your money isn't just a financial statement — it's a statement of values."

June 9 — Don't Chase Money — Attract It Through Value

"A worker is worthy of his wages." — Luke 10:7

Money should never be the primary target — it should be the natural result of providing value. When you obsess over chasing money, you become driven by scarcity, desperation, and short-term decisions. But when you focus on serving people well, solving real problems, and operating with excellence, income becomes a byproduct.

Money is drawn to value. When your leadership, service, creativity, wisdom, and integrity consistently help others, doors open. You don't have to manipulate; you simply have to become so effective that people *want* what you bring.

Chasing money leads to burnout and compromise. Becoming valuable leads to impact and reward. The question isn't, "How do I make more money?" It's, "How do I grow the value I bring to others?"

Reflection Questions

1. What problem do I solve better than most — and how can I grow that value?

2. Am I chasing income or building impact that naturally produces income?

Author Quote — Coach David Angeron

"Money follows value — not desperation."

June 10 — Financial Increase Begins With Order

You cannot grow what you refuse to organize. Financial chaos leads to financial stress. When your money has no structure — no budget, no plan, no tracking — it quietly leaks away, and with it goes your peace.

Before God increases your finances, He often calls you to increase your order. That means knowing what comes in, what goes out, where it goes, and why. When finances are organized:

- ◆ Stress decreases because you're not guessing
- ◆ Clarity increases because you see patterns
- ◆ Growth becomes possible because you can plan

Order prepares the way for overflow. It doesn't mean you have everything figured out — it means you're stewarding what you have with intention. God doesn't bless chaos; He blesses stewardship.

Reflection Questions

1. Where is financial disorder costing me peace or progress?

2. What system can I implement to create more financial clarity?

Author Quote — Coach David Angeron

"God doesn't bless chaos — He blesses stewardship."

June 11 — Don't Spend Like the Person You Are — Spend Like the Person You're Becoming

Your spending today is shaping your tomorrow. If you spend like the person you currently are — driven by mood, impulse, or pressure — you'll stay at your current level. If you spend like the person you're *becoming*, you'll begin to build a different future.

Financial maturity asks questions like:

♦ Does this purchase move me forward or hold me back?

♦ Am I living for status — or for strategy?

♦ Am I sacrificing long-term peace for short-term pleasure?

When you spend for image instead of impact, you trade future options for temporary impressions. Your spending should reflect your purpose — your calling, your goals, and your God-given assignment — not your need to impress people who don't run your race.

Reflection Questions

1. Do my financial decisions support my future or sabotage it?

2. What spending habit can I reduce or eliminate to accelerate growth?

Author Quote — Coach David Angeron

"If your spending doesn't match your future, your future will match your spending."

June 12 — Multiple Streams Build Stability

"Invest in seven ventures, yes, in eight." — Ecclesiastes 11:2

Dependence on a single source creates vulnerability. One job loss, one economic shift, one unexpected event can shake everything. God wants you wise, not worried — prepared, not panicked. Multiple income streams don't mean chasing everything; they mean building strategically.

Start with:

♦ One primary stream you develop with excellence
♦ Additional complementary streams you build gradually over time

This could be investments, side businesses, consulting, products, or creative work. The goal isn't greed — it's stability, generosity, and flexibility. When your income diversifies, your anxiety decreases and your capacity to bless others increases.

Multiple streams don't happen overnight, but they do happen on purpose.

Reflection Questions

1. What skill or opportunity could become an additional stream of income?

2. What financial step can I take to build long-term stability?

Author Quote — Coach David Angeron

"One stream pays the bills — multiple streams fund the calling."

JUNE 13 — YOUR NETWORK IMPACTS YOUR NET WORTH

"As iron sharpens iron, so one person sharpens another."
— Proverbs 27:17

Your financial mindset is heavily influenced by the people around you. Your circle will either normalize wisdom, discipline, and generosity — or normalize debt, impulse, and financial carelessness. You may not be able to choose every environment you're in, but you *can* be intentional about who speaks into your financial decisions.

Your financial circle matters:

- Spend time with savers, and you'll learn discipline
- Spend time with investors, and you'll learn strategy
- Spend time with reckless spenders, and you'll learn regret

The right relationships stretch your thinking, correct your blind spots, and model what's possible. The wrong ones subtly pull you into patterns that keep you stuck.

Your environment influences your economy more than you realize.

Reflection Questions

1. Does my circle strengthen or weaken my financial decisions?

2. Who can I learn from that has financial wisdom I need?

Author Quote — Coach David Angeron

"Your financial future rises when your environment raises its standards."

June 14 — Debt Is a Weight, Not a Weapon

"The borrower is slave to the lender." — Proverbs 22:7

Debt may offer convenience, but it quietly steals freedom. It delays dreams, restricts generosity, and places your future under someone else's timeline and terms. Debt is not always sinful — but it is always limiting.

The goal is not shame — it's strategy. You don't have to live under financial pressure forever. You can confront patterns, create a plan, reduce expenses, increase income, and attack debt step by step. Even slow progress toward freedom is still progress.

Debt-free is not just a financial condition — it's a leadership advantage. It frees your mind to think clearly, your heart to give generously, and your decisions to be driven by calling instead of creditors.

Reflection Questions

1. What spending habit or pattern has contributed most to financial pressure?

2. What step can I take today to begin reducing debt intentionally?

Author Quote — Coach David Angeron

"Debt offers convenience — discipline offers freedom."

June 15 — God Gives Ideas — Not Always Income

"He gives you the ability to produce wealth."
— Deuteronomy 8:18

When we pray for provision, we often expect immediate income. But God frequently answers with *ideas*, strategies, connections, and open doors. He gives you the *ability* to produce wealth — not just the wealth itself. That means creativity, insight, and innovation are part of His provision.

A God-idea left unacted upon is a blessing left unused. Many people are sitting on books, businesses, solutions, programs, inventions, or opportunities that never move past the "one day" stage. Ideas ignored become blessings delayed.

Start treating your ideas like assignments. Write them down. Pray over them. Seek counsel. Build a simple plan. Take one step. God is not asking you to finish it overnight — He's asking you to respond in faith.

Reflection Questions

1. What God-given idea have I neglected or procrastinated?

2. What is one step I can take this week to activate that idea?

Author Quote — Coach David Angeron

*"God's provision often arrives disguised as opportunity —
not currency."*

June 16 — Don't Compare Seasons — Steward Yours

"Let each one examine his own work." — Galatians 6:4

Comparison quietly kills financial progress. It shifts your focus from stewardship to insecurity. Instead of asking, "Lord, what do You want me to do with what I have?", comparison whispers, "Why don't I have what *they* have?" Everyone is in a different season. Some are in harvest, some in planting, some in pruning, and some in rebuilding. Someone else's visible abundance does not mean your journey is failing — it simply means their season is different.

God is not grading you based on someone else's progress report. He's looking at how you steward *your* opportunities, *your* income, *your* responsibilities, and *your* decisions. When you fixate on what others have, you stop noticing how far God has already brought you. Excellence increases finances — comparison decreases confidence. Gratitude fuels momentum because it reminds you that God is already at work.

Your financial journey is not behind — it's unique and being written on Heaven's timetable.

Reflection Questions

1. Where have I compared my journey to someone else's?

2. What progress can I celebrate instead of ignoring?

Author Quote — Coach David Angeron

"Comparison kills gratitude — and gratitude fuels momentum."

June 17 — Generosity Breaks the Grip of Greed

Greed whispers, "Hold tighter." The Kingdom whispers, "Give freely." Generosity doesn't weaken you — it strengthens you. It's evidence that money doesn't own your heart. Every time you give, you declare that God is your Source, not your paycheck, business, or bank account. God can get more resources to leaders who prove they'll let those resources flow through them.

Generosity doesn't require wealth — it requires willingness. You can be broke and generous. You can also be rich and stingy. God measures the heart behind the gift, not the size of the number. When generosity is a consistent part of your financial rhythm, you break the fear that says, "If I give, I won't have enough."

Generosity also keeps your motives pure. You stop chasing money for ego and start managing it for impact. The more you give, the more you realize how much God has already given you.

Reflection Questions

1. Is generosity a consistent part of my financial habits?

2. Who or what can I bless this week — even on a small scale?

Author Quote — Coach David Angeron

"We don't give because we have abundance — we gain abundance because we give."

June 18 — Wealth Is Built Slowly — Lost Quickly

"Steady plodding brings prosperity." — Proverbs 21:5 (TLB)

True wealth is not a lottery ticket — it's a lifestyle of discipline. It's built slowly through wise decisions, budgeting, saving, investing, and consistent work over time. Culture glorifies "fast money," but what comes quickly often leaves just as quickly. Hype, gambling, schemes, and shortcuts may promise speed, but they usually bring regret.

"Steady plodding" sounds boring, but it's powerful: paying down debt month by month, setting aside a percentage, saying no to unnecessary purchases, and learning as you go. Slow money grows strong because it's built on habits, not hype. It's rooted in stewardship, not impulse.

If it sounds too good to be true, it usually is. You don't need rushing — you need routine. Wealth is less about one big move and more about what you repeatedly do when no one is watching.

Reflection Questions

1. Am I pursuing shortcuts or building systems?
2. What daily or weekly discipline will make me wealthier long-term?

Author Quote — Coach David Angeron

"Wealth isn't a moment — it's a habit."

June 19 — Money Magnifies Who You Already Are

"From the overflow of the heart the mouth speaks." — Luke 6:45

Money doesn't transform character — it exposes and amplifies it. When resources increase, whatever is already inside a person gets louder. If there is generosity, more money will fuel greater giving. If there is selfishness, more money will fuel greater self-centeredness. If there is discipline, more money will support smarter decisions. If there is chaos, more money will create bigger messes.

This is why God takes character development so seriously. He knows that wealth is safest in the hands of the spiritually mature. He's not just preparing a financial future for you; He's preparing *you* for that financial future.

Before praying, "Lord, increase my income," it's wise to pray, "Lord, increase my integrity, self-control, and wisdom." The question is not only, "Can I get more?" but "Who am I becoming as God gives more?"

Reflection Questions

1. If my income doubled tomorrow, would my character support the increase?

2. What part of my heart needs God's shaping before wealth grows?

Author Quote — Coach David Angeron

"Money isn't a replacement for character — it's an amplifier of it."

JUNE 20 — BUILD WEALTH WITH PATIENCE, NOT PRESSURE

"Be still before the Lord and wait patiently for Him." — Psalm 37:7

Financial pressure can push leaders into dangerous decisions — risky investments, impulsive spending, shady partnerships, or shortcuts that compromise integrity. Anxiety says, "Hurry or you'll miss it." Wisdom says, "Wait, plan, and move with God." Patience is not passivity; it's controlled pace. It's trusting God's timing while still doing your part with diligence.

Fast money often fades because it was built on urgency, not understanding. Patient money lasts because it's built on education, strategy, and consistent effort. God isn't just interested in you "getting ahead" — He's interested in you staying free.

Ask yourself: am I chasing quick relief or long-term stability? Building wealth with patience means saying "no" to the pressure to keep up appearances and "yes" to the slower, stronger path of wise stewardship.

Reflection Questions

1. Where am I making financial decisions based on urgency rather than wisdom?

2. How can I slow down and practice patience in my financial planning?

Author Quote — Coach David Angeron

"Blessings gained slowly are enjoyed fully — blessings rushed are regretted quickly."

June 21 —
The Goal Is Freedom, Not Flexing

The world uses money to show off — God calls leaders to use money to *show up*. Culture pushes you to buy the car, the clothes, the house, and the lifestyle that proves you "made it." But true success is not about flexing something temporary; it's about building something eternal.

Buying status feels good for a moment. Buying freedom feels good for a lifetime. Freedom means living without constant financial stress, without heavy debt, and with the ability to say "yes" when God asks you to give, go, or build. Freedom means time to be present with your family and capacity to fund what matters most.

Ask yourself honestly: do I want wealth for purpose or for applause? Financial decisions rooted in image will always leave you empty. Financial decisions rooted in purpose create peace and legacy.

Reflection Questions

1. Do I want wealth for purpose or for applause?

2. Which financial choice right now will bring more long-term freedom?

Author Quote — Coach David Angeron

"Status impresses people — financial freedom impacts generations."

June 22 — Never Let Money Lead Your Decisions

Money is an excellent servant but a terrible master. When it becomes the primary driver of your decisions, calling gets sacrificed on the altar of comfort. Jobs are chosen purely for salary, not assignment. Opportunities are rejected because they don't pay enough immediately, even if they align with God's purpose.

God is not asking you to be careless with finances — He is asking you to be led by Him, not by fear of lack or obsession with more. When God leads and money follows, provision becomes a blessing. When money leads and you ask God to follow, it becomes bondage.

Sometimes the door that pays less today develops you more for tomorrow. Sometimes the obedient "yes" looks financially smaller in the moment but spiritually massive in the long run. Purpose must make the decision; money can show up later.

Reflection Questions

1. Have I avoided an opportunity because it paid less but aligned more with purpose?

2. Where do I need to trust God rather than financial comfort?

Author Quote — Coach David Angeron

*"Don't let money make decisions —
let purpose make decisions and money will follow."*

June 23 — Don't Pray for Harvest If You Fear Work

"The lazy do not roast any game, but the diligent feed on the riches of the hunt."
— Proverbs 12:27

Everyone loves the idea of harvest — financial breakthrough, business growth, debt freedom, abundance. But harvest is heavy. It requires work. Fields don't reap themselves. Opportunities don't manage themselves. Wealth doesn't organize or steward itself.

God will bless the work of your hands, not the wishes of your heart. Prayer is powerful — but prayer is never a substitute for discipline, labor, and follow-through. If you ask God for abundance but resist effort, you're praying for results without responsibility.

The diligent "roast their game" — they finish what they start. They do the unglamorous tasks, manage the details, call the clients, track the finances, and stay with it long after excitement fades. Harvest belongs to those hungry enough to work for it.

Reflection Questions

1. Where do I expect reward without the required work?

2. What effort do I need to intensify to see greater results?

Author Quote — Coach David Angeron

"The harvest belongs to those hungry enough to work for it."

June 24 — Your Daily Decisions Shape Your Destiny

"Whoever gathers money little by little makes it grow." — Proverbs 13:11

Destiny is not built in one big, dramatic moment — it's forged through hundreds of small, often unseen decisions. Financial health doesn't come from a single bonus, a single deal, or a single raise. It comes from "little by little" — saving a bit each month, saying no to unnecessary debt, learning consistently, and making wiser choices day after day.

Your daily choices are either moving you closer to financial peace or further from it. The coffee, the subscription, the impulse buy, the ignored budget — they all stack up. So do the consistent investments, the small acts of discipline, and the careful planning.

Intentions don't shape destiny — habits do. The good news is you don't have to fix everything overnight. You just have to start making better decisions today and repeat them tomorrow.

Reflection Questions

1. What daily habit is moving me closer to financial peace?
2. What daily habit is moving me away from it?

Author Quote — Coach David Angeron

"Small decisions repeated daily lead to massive results eventually."

JUNE 25 — DON'T SPEND TO ESCAPE EMOTIONS

"Self-control is better than conquering a city." — Proverbs 16:32

One of the sneakiest financial traps is emotional spending. We don't swipe the card because we need something — we swipe because we want to feel something. Celebration shopping, stress shopping, sadness shopping, boredom shopping — all create a temporary high and long-term regret.

Emotions should be processed, not purchased. When spending becomes your coping mechanism, money starts medicating what only God and healthy community can heal. Financial maturity doesn't mean you never enjoy your money; it means you don't use it to numb pain, impress others, or escape reality.

Ask yourself before big purchases: "Am I buying this for purpose — or for comfort, image, or distraction?" Self-control in your emotions creates self-control in your expenses. Leaders who can't manage their feelings will never manage their finances well.

Reflection Questions

1. Do I buy to celebrate, distract, numb, or impress?
2. What emotion triggers my weakest financial decisions?

Author Quote — Coach David Angeron

"Uncontrolled emotions lead to uncontrolled expenses."

June 26 — God Uses Generosity to Open Doors Money Can't

"A generous person will prosper." — Proverbs 11:25

Money can buy access — but generosity builds favor. Transactions are temporary; generosity is remembered. When you give as God leads — to people, ministries, missions, or needs — you step into a different economy: Heaven's.

Sometimes the breakthrough you're praying for isn't on the other side of more *earning* — it's on the other side of more *sowing*. God uses generosity to open doors that discounts, negotiation, or strategy never could. It softens hearts, builds trust, and creates relationships where you're seen as a blessing, not just a taker.

Generosity doesn't always produce an instant financial return, but it always produces spiritual and relational impact. And in the long run, God knows how to route provision back to the hands that freely give.

Reflection Questions

1. When have I felt God nudge me to give and ignored it?
2. Who can I bless this week as an act of obedience?

Author Quote — Coach David Angeron

"Money can open doors — generosity can open hearts."

JUNE 27 — OPPORTUNITIES MULTIPLY FOR THE DILIGENT

"Do you see someone skilled in their work? They will stand before kings."
— Proverbs 22:29

Some people pray for opportunities while others prepare as if opportunity is inevitable. Diligence is the bridge between where you are and the rooms you want to be in. When you consistently show up with excellence — even when the room looks small — the right people eventually hear about you.

Excellence makes your name travel farther than your voice. You don't need to push your way into every space; your work can speak for you. Leaders who are diligent in hidden seasons are often promoted in public ones. The world may call it "luck," but Heaven calls it stewardship.

Ask yourself: If the opportunity I'm praying for showed up tomorrow, would my skills, systems, and discipline be ready — or exposed?

Reflection Questions

1. Am I preparing as if greater opportunity is guaranteed?
2. What skill, habit, or discipline would triple my opportunities if sharpened?

Author Quote — Coach David Angeron

"Opportunity always looks for the prepared — not the popular."

June 28 — Wealth Is Not Just What You Earn — It's What You Keep

"A fool spends all he has." — Proverbs 21:20

High income is not the same as high wealth. Plenty of people earn impressive money but live under constant financial pressure because everything they receive immediately flows out. Income creates possibility — stewardship turns that possibility into stability.

Wealth grows when you keep, save, and invest a portion of what comes in — not when you constantly upgrade your lifestyle. If your expenses rise every time your income rises, you'll run forever without feeling secure. You cannot out-earn poor stewardship.

Ask yourself: Does my lifestyle grow faster than my wisdom? Am I more focused on appearing successful than building true stability? Real wealth is quiet, patient, and strategic.

Reflection Questions

1. Does my lifestyle grow faster than my wisdom?
2. What percentage of my income should I save or invest — and what's stopping me?

Author Quote — Coach David Angeron

"Earning makes you money — stewardship keeps it."

June 29 — Don't Increase Lifestyle Faster Than Discipline

There's a subtle danger in rising income: the temptation to inflate lifestyle faster than you inflate discipline. New money often invites new toys — cars, clothes, trips, subscriptions, upgrades. None of these are wrong by themselves, but when lifestyle grows faster than wisdom, the result is stress, not freedom.

Wealth doesn't come from simply earning more — it comes from controlling more. The goal isn't to look rich; it's to be stable, secure, debt-free, and generous. It's to build a life that isn't one paycheck or one crisis away from collapse.

When income increases, ask first:

♦ How can I increase giving?
♦ How can I increase saving or investing?
♦ How can I increase margin and freedom?

Then consider lifestyle changes. Let discipline rise before lifestyle does.

Reflection Questions

1. Has my lifestyle elevated faster than my financial discipline?

2. What change today will create more long-term stability?

Author Quote — Coach David Angeron

"If your discipline doesn't grow with your income, your income won't stay."

June 30 — Leave a Legacy, Not Just an Income

Income sustains your present — legacy shapes your future generations. God doesn't just want you to break cycles for yourself; He wants you to break them for those who come after you. Legacy is more than money, but it absolutely includes financial wisdom, resources, and structures that outlive you.

A legacy is built when:

♦ You steward resources wisely instead of recklessly

♦ You teach your children (and spiritual children) how to handle money God's way

♦ You invest in purposes, people, and projects that will keep bearing fruit after you're gone

Ask yourself: Am I only trying to "make it," or am I building something that won't collapse when I'm no longer here? Legacy is leadership extended beyond your lifetime — your faith, values, and stewardship continuing to speak long after you're done speaking.

Reflection Questions

1. Am I building wealth only for today — or for the future?

2. What can I put in place now that will benefit the next generation?

Author Quote — Coach David Angeron

"Income is temporary — legacy is generational."

192

JULY

WISDOM, DECISION-MAKING & DIVINE STRATEGY

July 1 — Leaders Are Called to Be Courageous

"Be strong and courageous... for the Lord your God is with you." — Joshua 1:9

Leadership will always demand courage — never just comfort. Courage is the willingness to step into uncertainty with full obedience, even when you can't predict the outcome. It shows up when you walk into difficult meetings, make unpopular decisions, uphold standards others ignore, and lead in directions people don't yet understand. God never promised leaders an easy path — He promised His presence on the path.

Courage is not the absence of fear; it's the refusal to bow to it. Fear says, "What if this goes wrong?" Courage says, "What if God moves because I obeyed?" Courageous leaders remember who sent them. They know they don't walk into any room, decision, or battle alone. When God is with you, you don't have to feel fearless — you just have to move forward in faith.

Your calling is bigger than your comfort. Lead like God is standing right beside you — because He is.

Reflection Questions

1. What decision have I avoided because it feels uncomfortable?

2. Where is God calling me to lead boldly right now?

Author Quote — Coach David Angeron

"Courage is not a feeling — it is leadership in motion."

JULY 2 — LEADERS DO HARD THINGS

"Do what is right and good in the Lord's sight." — Deuteronomy 6:18

Leadership is not about choosing what's easy — it's about choosing what's right. Hard decisions are where leadership is truly revealed. Leaders confront what others avoid: toxic behavior, underperformance, broken systems, misalignment, and difficult conversations. They make decisions that protect mission over comfort, values over popularity, and long-term health over short-term relief.

Easy choices build weak leaders because they require no sacrifice. Hard choices build strong leaders because they demand conviction, clarity, and courage. The decisions you delay don't disappear — they compound into bigger problems. Every time you face what's uncomfortable, you grow in strength, credibility, and trust.

Doing hard things doesn't mean you stop feeling the weight — it means you carry it anyway for the sake of those you lead. The greatest leaders weren't the most comfortable — they were the most committed to doing what's right, no matter the cost.

Reflection Questions

1. What tough decision am I avoiding that is costing progress?

2. What immediate action will move the team and mission forward?

Author Quote — Coach David Angeron

"If you avoid what's hard, you avoid what matters."

July 3 — Confidence Comes From Calling, Not Approval

If your confidence is built on applause, it will crumble under pressure. People's opinions are unstable — supportive one moment, critical the next. True confidence comes from knowing who called you, not how many people approve of you. When you know God assigned you to a task, room, or position, you stop begging people to validate what Heaven already confirmed.

Leadership means following God's direction even when critics are louder than cheerleaders. Sometimes you will be misunderstood, questioned, or underestimated. That doesn't mean you're out of place — it often means you're ahead of them. Confidence built on calling says, "I may not have everyone's approval, but I have God's assignment — and that's enough."

You are not validated by applause — you are authorized by purpose. Lead like someone who was placed, not someone who is merely permitted.

Reflection Questions

1. Where have I been seeking approval instead of obeying calling?

2. How would I lead differently if I cared less about opinions?

Author Quote — Coach David Angeron

"You are not confident because people approve of you — you are confident because God assigned you."

July 4 — Bold Decisions Require Clear Identity

"You are a chosen people." — 1 Peter 2:9

Timid leadership is often rooted in an unclear identity. When you forget who you are in Christ — chosen, called, loved, and equipped — every decision feels fragile. You second-guess your instincts, overthink your choices, and hesitate when God is prompting you to move.

But when your identity is anchored in God's truth, boldness rises. You remember you are not leading alone, not guessing your way forward, not accidentally in the position you're in. Security in identity produces security in decision-making. You stop leading to prove yourself and start leading from the truth of who you already are.

The enemy attacks identity because he knows if he shakes your identity, he can shake your decisions. You must constantly remind yourself: I am chosen. I am assigned. I am equipped. From that place, you can make bold, clear decisions that align with Heaven, not insecurity.

Reflection Questions

1. What lie about myself weakens my confidence?

2. What truth about my God-given identity needs to guide my leadership?

Author Quote — Coach David Angeron

"Bold leadership starts with secure identity."

July 5 — Don't Fear Standing Alone

"The gate is narrow and the road is difficult." — Matthew 7:14

There will be moments when leadership feels lonely. When you hold a higher standard, others may label you strict. When you protect values over convenience, people may question your decisions. When you refuse to compromise integrity, some will distance themselves. Standing alone doesn't make you wrong — it often makes you early.

Leaders are called to walk narrow roads — paths others will appreciate later but resist in the moment. History honors those who stood firm when it was unpopular: the coach who protected culture, the boss who refused shady shortcuts, the entrepreneur who stayed ethical when it cost money.

You cannot lead effectively if you're terrified of standing apart. Your job is not to blend in — it's to obey God, even if you're the only one in the room doing it. In time, results and fruit will speak louder than the loneliness ever did.

Reflection Questions

1. Where do I need to stand firm even if I stand alone?
2. What fear of disapproval is holding my leadership back?

Author Quote — Coach David Angeron

"The path to greatness is rarely crowded."

July 6 —
Clarity Requires Saying "No"

Most leaders aren't overwhelmed because they lack opportunities — they're overwhelmed because they lack boundaries. Every yes is a promise of your time, energy, mental capacity, and emotional bandwidth. If you say yes to everything, you eventually say no to excellence, health, and clarity.

Saying no is not selfish — it's strategic. It protects your calling from being diluted by distractions. Great leaders understand they are stewards of their assignment, not servants to everyone's demands. They ask, "Does this align with my mission? Does this deserve my best energy?"

Busyness is not the same as effectiveness. You can be busy all day and still move nowhere. Clarity comes when you courageously say no to what doesn't fit, so you can fully say yes to what God actually called you to build.

Reflection Questions

1. What do I need to say "no" to in order to say "yes" to my calling?
2. Where have I confused busyness with effectiveness?

Author Quote — Coach David Angeron

"Saying yes builds opportunities — saying no protects them."

JULY 7 — PROGRESS REQUIRES PRESSURE

"Suffering produces perseverance; perseverance, character; and character, hope."
— Romans 5:3–4

A life without pressure rarely produces a leader with power. Pressure is uncomfortable, but it is also productive. It develops resilience, emotional strength, and spiritual maturity. The muscles you need to carry greater influence are built in seasons where you're stretched, tested, and pushed beyond what feels easy.

God doesn't use pressure to punish you — He uses it to prepare you. The situations you wish would disappear are often the ones developing your capacity to lead at the next level. Pressure in relationships teaches communication. Pressure in finances teaches stewardship. Pressure in leadership teaches wisdom and dependence on God.

Instead of always praying, "Lord, remove this," sometimes the better prayer is, "Lord, use this." Progress is born in perseverance. The leaders who impact the most are rarely the ones who had the least pressure — they're the ones who let God use it.

Reflection Questions

1. What pressure is God using to build strength in me right now?

2. Instead of praying for relief, should I pray for resilience?

Author Quote — Coach David Angeron

"Pressure doesn't block progress — it builds it."

July 8 — Leadership Requires Taking the First Step Before You See the Second

"We walk by faith, not by sight." — 2 Corinthians 5:7

Leadership rarely comes with full blueprints. God usually gives you a direction, not a detailed itinerary. If you wait until every detail is clear before you move, you'll stay stuck wishing while others build. Faith-filled leadership is taking the step you can see and trusting God to reveal the next one at the right time.

You don't need a ten-year plan to obey today's instruction. Start the program. Make the call. Launch the idea. Have the conversation. Apply for the opportunity. You learn, adjust, and refine as you move. God steers moving ships, not anchored ones.

Obedience today unlocks clarity tomorrow. The second step often won't appear until you've taken the first. Trust that the God who called you sees the full path. Your job isn't to control the journey — it's to walk faithfully in the light you have now.

Reflection Questions

1. What action have I postponed because I wanted more certainty first?

2. What step of obedience is God calling me to take today?

Author Quote — Coach David Angeron

"Leaders don't need full clarity to move — they need full faith."

July 9 — The Hard Road Leads to Higher Ground

The hardest seasons of your life are often the most defining ones. The easy road keeps you comfortable, but the hard road shapes your character, convictions, and capacity. Most people turn back when the path gets steep — leaders lean in, trusting that God is using the climb for something greater.

The presence of resistance is not always a sign to stop; sometimes it's proof that you're walking a path worth fighting for. The enemy doesn't resist what doesn't matter. The frustration, criticism, and obstacles may actually be confirming that you're stepping toward higher ground.

God doesn't abandon you on the hard road — He meets you there. He delivers, strengthens, and refines you in the process. Don't assume difficulty means detour. Sometimes the hard road *is* the exact route to destiny.

Reflection Questions

1. Where have I been tempted to quit simply because the path is hard?

2. What if the struggle is the very proof that breakthrough is near?

Author Quote — Coach David Angeron

"The hard road doesn't block destiny — it leads to it."

July 10 — Courage Isn't Loud — It's Consistent

"Stand firm in the faith; be courageous; be strong." — 1 Corinthians 16:13

Courage is often pictured as a single, loud, heroic moment. But in real leadership, courage usually looks quieter: showing up again after a tough week, holding the line on values, making the wise decision instead of the easy one, and staying faithful when emotions are low.

Courage is commitment in the face of difficulty. It's not just what you declare in big moments — it's what you do day after day when no spotlight is on you. The strongest leaders are not necessarily the loudest; they are the ones who keep moving in the right direction, even when they feel tired, misunderstood, or unseen.

Courageous leadership is less about hype and more about habits. It's the pattern of saying, "I will not back down from what God called me to," regardless of how you feel. Over time, that steady courage creates undeniable impact.

Reflection Questions

1. Is my courage visible only in emotion, or also in consistency?

2. Where do I need to keep showing up even when motivation fades?

Author Quote — Coach David Angeron

"Courage isn't proven by moments — it's proven by patterns."

July 11 — Leaders Face Conflict Directly

Avoiding conflict doesn't create unity — it quietly destroys it. When leaders ignore issues, resentment grows in the shadows. Performance drops, trust erodes, and culture weakens while everyone pretends everything is fine. Healthy leadership means facing conflict head-on, but with wisdom, humility, and respect.

You can't create peace by pretending problems don't exist. You create peace by addressing them with clarity and love. Direct conversations may feel uncomfortable in the moment, but they protect the mission and the relationship long-term. Conflict handled correctly actually builds trust — people know where they stand and understand expectations.

Leaders who face conflict honor both people and purpose. They don't explode in anger or hide in silence. They communicate clearly, listen sincerely, and move toward resolution. That's how mature teams are built.

Reflection Questions

1. What conflict am I avoiding because it's uncomfortable?

2. How can I approach it with clarity, humility, and maturity?

Author Quote — Coach David Angeron

"Avoiding conflict protects feelings — confronting conflict protects the mission."

JULY 12 —
IF YOU WANT LOYALTY, BE LOYAL

L oyalty is not something you demand — it's something you model. People are far more likely to stand with a leader who has stood with them. When you believe in your people, back them publicly, support them privately, and refuse to throw them under the bus when things get tough, you build a culture of mutual loyalty.

Loyalty doesn't mean ignoring accountability. It means you correct without condemning and challenge without abandoning. It means you see people's potential even when they stumble. Leaders who only expect loyalty but never show it create fear, not commitment.

If you want teams that will fight for the mission, show them you're willing to fight for *them*. Celebrate their wins, defend them when they're not in the room, and stay consistent when pressure rises. Trust and loyalty will grow from there.

Reflection Questions

1. Do I demonstrate loyalty, or do I only expect it from others?

2. Who on my team needs to feel seen, supported, or valued this week?

Author Quote — Coach David Angeron

"You earn loyalty by giving it."

July 13 — Stop Explaining Yourself to People Who Are Committed to Misunderstanding You

"Do not answer a fool according to his folly." — Proverbs 26:4

Not everyone deserves an explanation. Some people don't want understanding — they want argument. Some aren't interested in truth — they're invested in control, drama, or criticism. When you spend your energy constantly defending yourself to the wrong people, you're draining strength that belongs to your assignment.

Wisdom is knowing the difference between someone who is genuinely confused and someone who is committed to misunderstanding you. One needs clarity; the other thrives on chaos. Your purpose cannot run at full speed if you keep stopping to persuade people who never intended to support you.

Let your results speak. Let your character speak. Let time and fruit speak. Your job is to obey God, serve people, and steward the vision — not convince every critic that you're called.

Reflection Questions

1. Whose opinion am I giving too much power in my life?

2. How much stronger would I be if I stopped trying to convince the wrong people?

Author Quote — Coach David Angeron

"Stop explaining yourself to critics — your results will speak for you."

July 14 — Leaders Take Responsibility — Not Blame

"Each of us will give an account of ourselves to God." — Romans 14:12

Blame looks outward; responsibility looks inward. Blame says, "It's their fault." Responsibility says, "What can I learn? What can I adjust? How can I lead differently?" Weak leaders protect their ego by shifting blame to people, circumstances, or timing. Strong leaders protect progress by owning their part.

Taking responsibility doesn't mean everything is your fault — it means everything is your opportunity. When you take ownership, you regain power to change. When you stay stuck in blame, you surrender that power and delay growth.

Godly leadership recognizes that every situation is a classroom. Mistakes, miscommunications, missed goals — all become fuel for development when you approach them with ownership instead of excuses. Responsibility accelerates your growth and your team's trust.

Reflection Questions

1. Where have I blamed circumstances instead of taking ownership?

2. What decision today would move me from excuse to responsibility?

Author Quote — Coach David Angeron

"Blame protects ego — responsibility protects progress."

July 15 — Leaders Apologize When Necessary

Real leaders don't pretend to be flawless — they practice being honest. Apology is not a sign of weakness; it's a sign of maturity and security. People follow leaders who can admit when they were wrong, misinformed, impatient, or unfair. They respect humility far more than perfect image management.

An apology restores trust faster than excuses ever will. It tells your team, "I value this relationship and this mission more than my pride." It sets a culture where honesty is normal and where people feel safe owning their own mistakes too.

Apologizing doesn't lower your authority — it deepens it. It shows that your integrity matters more than your appearance. Leaders who never apologize end up isolated. Leaders who apologize appropriately build loyalty, unity, and long-term credibility.

Reflection Questions

1. Is there anyone I need to apologize to for the sake of unity and leadership integrity?

2. What fear keeps me from admitting when I'm wrong?

Author Quote — Coach David Angeron

"A real leader would rather be humble than be right."

July 16 — Leaders Don't Need Permission to Lead

"Do not neglect the gift that is in you." — 1 Timothy 4:14

If you wait for permission to lead, you'll wait your whole life. Leadership is not something others grant you — it's something you choose to walk in. God has already placed gifts, insight, vision, and conviction inside you. Titles may come later, recognition may come later, platforms may come later — but leadership begins the moment you take responsibility for what God placed in your hands.

Leaders don't sit around hoping someone notices them. They notice what's broken and start building. They see what's missing and start serving. They hear from God and move before the crowd understands. Waiting for universal approval kills more callings than failure ever will.

You are not disqualified because people haven't announced you yet. Heaven already did. If God trusted you with a gift, He expects you to use it — not hide it until others applaud it. Start where you are, with what you have, and let God validate what He initiated.

Reflection Questions

1. Where have I been qualified by God but waiting on validation from people?

2. What action should I take instead of waiting for permission?

Author Quote — Coach David Angeron

"A calling that needs permission is no longer a calling — it's insecurity."

July 17 — When God Says Move, Move

"Obedience is better than sacrifice." — 1 Samuel 15:22

Delayed obedience is disobedience disguised as caution. When God gives direction, He's not just suggesting a good idea — He's inviting you into alignment with His timing, favor, and strategy. Doors often open in specific seasons, and those seasons don't last forever. You can pray, plan, and prepare, but at some point, God will say, "Now." When He does, your responsibility is not to negotiate — it's to move.

Many leaders are stuck not because they lack ability, but because they delayed obedience. They overanalyzed, hesitated, polled opinions, and watched momentum drift away. Breakthrough often sits on the other side of the decision you keep postponing.

Obedience may feel risky, but it's the safest place you can stand — in the middle of God's will. You don't need all the answers to move; you need enough faith to act on what you already know God said.

Reflection Questions

1. Has God prompted me to do something that I've delayed?
2. What step will I take today — not someday?

Author Quote — Coach David Angeron

"The longer you delay obedience, the more expensive it becomes."

July 18 — Leaders Grow Through Feedback, Not Flattery

"Wounds from a friend can be trusted." — Proverbs 27:6

Flattery feels good in the moment, but it doesn't make you better. Growth requires truth — especially the uncomfortable kind. Leaders who only surround themselves with people who praise them eventually plateau. Leaders who intentionally invite correction, coaching, and honest evaluation become sharper, wiser, and more effective over time.

Feedback is not an attack on your identity; it's an investment in your development. Trusted voices can see blind spots you miss: patterns in your leadership, tone, decisions, or pace that may eventually cause damage if not adjusted. Wise leaders don't just tolerate feedback — they seek it, thank people for it, and apply it.

You don't need critics tearing you down, but you *do* need truth-tellers who love you enough to challenge you. Let your ego feel the sting so your leadership can experience the growth. In the long run, feedback is a gift that flattery can never replace.

Reflection Questions

1. Do I welcome honest feedback or avoid it because it's uncomfortable?

2. Who can I invite to speak truth into my leadership?

Author Quote — Coach David Angeron

"Flattery feeds pride — feedback feeds growth."

211

July 19 — Don't Fear the Weight of Responsibility

"To whom much is given, much will be required." — Luke 12:48

Leadership is heavy because what you carry matters. The weight you feel — decisions, people, culture, finances, outcomes — isn't a sign that you're failing; it's evidence that you've been entrusted with something significant. God doesn't place influence in the hands of those who refuse responsibility. He trusts those who are willing to carry it with Him.

The goal is not to escape responsibility, but to steward it without being crushed by it. Burnout often comes when leaders try to carry the weight alone, in their own strength, for their own glory. Purpose rises when leaders remember they are stewards, not saviors. God didn't call you to be superhuman — He called you to rely on His strength while you walk in yours.

Instead of resenting responsibility, reframe it: "This weight proves I'm trusted. It proves this matters." Let that awareness drive you back to God's grace, not to exhaustion.

Reflection Questions

1. What responsibility have I been resenting instead of embracing?
2. How can I shift from burnout to purpose in how I view responsibility?

Author Quote — Coach David Angeron

"The weight you carry is proof you're trusted with something that matters."

July 20 — Leadership Requires Decisiveness

"Let your 'Yes' be 'Yes,' and your 'No,' be 'No.'" — Matthew 5:37

Indecision is one of the quiet killers of momentum. When leaders hesitate endlessly, teams stall, confidence drops, and opportunities pass by. Perfect clarity almost never arrives — at some point, you must decide based on prayer, wisdom, and the best information you have.

No decision is often worse than a wrong decision. Wrong decisions can be corrected, learned from, and adjusted. No decision leaves everyone stuck, confused, and uncertain. Decisive leaders bring direction, even in imperfect circumstances. They understand that leadership requires risk — and that failure, when submitted to God, becomes education.

Decisiveness doesn't mean recklessness. It means you seek counsel, pray, weigh options — and then *move*. Every time you make a clear decision, you strengthen your leadership muscles and your team's trust.

Reflection Questions

1. What decision have I postponed that needs clarity today?

2. What small step can break the cycle of hesitation?

Author Quote — Coach David Angeron

"Indecision is a decision — and it always chooses failure."

July 21 — Big Decisions Require Big Faith

"With God all things are possible." — Matthew 19:26

If the vision came from God, it will always be bigger than what you can accomplish alone. God-sized assignments stretch beyond your experience, resources, comfort, and natural capacity. That's intentional — so you must lean on Him instead of your own strength.

Big decisions can't be made on human logic alone. If you only move when everything adds up on paper, you'll miss moments where God wants to show His power. Faith doesn't ignore wisdom; it elevates it by trusting that God can make a way where you see none.

Every major move in your calling will bring a choice: trust God or retreat into safety. Big faith doesn't mean you stop planning — it means your plan includes room for God to do what only He can do. If you can fully do it without Him, it may be a project, but it's not a God-sized vision.

Reflection Questions

1. Where am I depending on human limitation instead of God's provision?
2. What big decision will require me to trust God at a new level?

Author Quote — Coach David Angeron

"If you can do it without God, then it's not God-sized."

July 22 — Lead With Conviction, Not Consensus

Leaders who chase consensus rarely carry true conviction. If every decision must be unanimously approved, you'll end up watering down vision to keep everyone comfortable. Conviction is the inner knowing that you are obeying God, even when people don't fully understand or agree.

Consensus isn't always bad — collaboration and counsel matter. But when pleasing people begins to outrank honoring God, leadership is compromised. Conviction says, "I'd rather obey God and be misunderstood than disobey Him and be applauded."

Culture is loud. Opinions are constant. Criticism is guaranteed. The question is: what voice leads your decisions? Conviction anchored in God's Word keeps you steady when trends shift, pressure rises, and people waffle. You're not called to be a people-pleaser — you're called to be a purpose-keeper.

Reflection Questions

1. Am I making decisions based on conviction or fear of criticism?

2. What decision aligns with purpose even if others don't understand it yet?

Author Quote — Coach David Angeron

"If conviction doesn't lead the decision, culture will."

July 23 — A Leader's Calling Will Be Misunderstood

Sometimes the people who know your past struggle most to see your future. Familiarity can blind people to your growth, maturity, and calling. They remember your mistakes, your immaturity, your previous version — and they freeze you there in their minds.

If you're not careful, you'll shrink to fit their memory instead of stretching to fit God's vision. Being misunderstood is not a sign that you missed God — often, it's proof that He's moving you into new territory. Those who only know the "old you" may never fully understand the "called you."

You are not obligated to dim your calling to make others comfortable with your growth. Keep leading, building, and obeying. In time, fruit will speak louder than familiarity. Some will eventually understand. Others never will. Your assignment is to honor God with your calling, not convince everyone to agree with it.

Reflection Questions

1. Where have I allowed misunderstanding to make me smaller?

2. How would I lead differently if others' opinions didn't shape my confidence?

Author Quote — Coach David Angeron

"Some people can't see who you are becoming because they only remember who you were."

July 24 — The Right Decision Is Usually the Hard Decision

"Enter through the narrow gate." — Matthew 7:13

Right decisions rarely feel easy in the moment. They may cost you comfort, convenience, relationships, or short-term gain. Wrong decisions often feel easier because they offer quick relief and delayed consequences. But ease and effectiveness are rarely the same thing.

The narrow gate represents the path that is harder to walk but better to live with. Choosing integrity over compromise, discipline over laziness, confrontation over avoidance, and long-term vision over short-term relief is rarely fun at first — but it produces peace, respect, and results.

Leaders must think beyond today's feelings and into tomorrow's fruit. Ask yourself, "What choice aligns with who God is calling me to become?" The right decision is often the one that stretches you, challenges you, and requires sacrifice — but your future self will thank you for it.

Reflection Questions

1. What decision feels hard but right?
2. What would future-me thank present-me for choosing?

Author Quote — Coach David Angeron

"Easy choices bring regret — hard choices bring results."

July 25 — Don't Expect People Without Vision to Support Big Vision

"Where there is no vision, the people perish." — Proverbs 29:18

Big vision can feel threatening to small thinking. Some people can't grasp what God showed you because He didn't show it to them. Their lack of excitement is not proof your vision is wrong — it may just be proof that it's bigger than their current perspective.

You can't expect those without vision to carry the weight of yours. Their doubt, fear, or skepticism doesn't disqualify your calling. Stop wasting energy trying to persuade those who were never assigned to the building process. Vision needs carriers — people who see it, believe in it, and are willing to sacrifice for it.

Ask God to highlight who is truly called to help you build. Invest more energy into equipping the committed than arguing with the unconvinced. The right people will not only support the vision — they'll help multiply it.

Reflection Questions

1. Whose doubt or small mindset has been influencing my confidence?

2. Who truly believes in the mission — and how can I empower them more?

Author Quote — Coach David Angeron

"Vision needs carriers — not critics."

July 26 — Critics Don't Build — Leaders Do

"By their fruit you will know them." — Matthew 7:16

Critics are loud — but fruit is louder. Critics talk about what should be done; leaders roll up their sleeves and do it. Critics analyze from the sidelines; leaders step onto the field. Criticism is easy, cheap, and often detached from responsibility. Leadership costs something.

You don't prove critics wrong by debating them — you prove them wrong by building what God called you to build and letting results speak. Over time, the difference between a critic and a leader is obvious: one leaves comments, the other leaves impact.

It's wise to evaluate honest critique, but it's foolish to be paralyzed by noise. Ask yourself: Does this person have fruit? Do they carry responsibility? Are they invested in the mission? If not, their words shouldn't weigh more than your assignment.

Reflection Questions

1. Have I spent more energy listening to critics than building?

2. What action will silence doubt more than any explanation?

Author Quote — Coach David Angeron

"Critics write commentary — leaders write history."

JULY 27 — REAL LEADERS DON'T QUIT WHEN IT GETS LONELY

"I am with you always." — Matthew 28:20

Leadership can feel lonely — not because God abandoned you, but because the path you're walking is narrower than most. Responsibility separates you. Conviction separates you. Vision separates you. Before God elevates you, He often allows seasons where you stand with fewer people so you can learn to stand more deeply with Him.

Loneliness is not always a signal to quit — sometimes it's proof you're being prepared. In these seasons, God strengthens your dependence on Him instead of the crowd. He purifies your motives, clarifies your vision, and builds resilience that popularity could never provide.

You are not truly alone — Heaven is still in the room. Angels don't post on social, but they still surround you. God doesn't leave you when the room clears out. Keep leading, keep building, and let God turn lonely seasons into launching seasons.

Reflection Questions

1. Where has loneliness made me question my calling?

2. What if this season is developing strength, not isolation?

Author Quote — Coach David Angeron

"Leadership will isolate you before it elevates you."

July 28 — Vision Requires Endurance, Not Emotion

"Let us run with endurance the race set before us." — Hebrews 12:1

Emotion may start the race, but only endurance finishes it. You won't always *feel* inspired, energized, or excited about the vision. There will be days where fatigue, discouragement, or frustration hit hard. That's when leaders discover whether they were fueled by hype or anchored by calling.

Endurance doesn't mean you never get tired — it means you keep going with wisdom. You rest but don't resign. You adjust but don't abandon. You remember why God called you, not just how you currently feel about it.

Great visions often outlive emotional highs. That's why routines, disciplines, and systems matter. They carry you when feelings don't. The leaders who make the deepest impact aren't the most emotional — they're the most faithful.

Reflection Questions

1. What area of my calling requires endurance right now?

2. What routine or habit will sustain my strength when motivation is low?

Author Quote — Coach David Angeron

"Dreams are started by emotion — destinies are finished by endurance."

July 29 — Protect the Vision From Vision Killers

Not everyone around you is safe for the vision within you. Vision killers don't always look obvious — they can be negative attitudes, constant criticism, gossip, laziness, jealousy, or subtle cynicism. Over time, these voices weaken conviction, drain energy, and dilute passion.

As a leader, you are responsible not just for casting vision, but for *protecting* it. That means honoring those who build, challenge in love those who drift, and, when necessary, releasing those who persistently undermine the mission. Mercy doesn't mean giving people unlimited permission to poison culture.

You can't build with people who secretly hope you lose or who consistently resist what God is asking you to create. Surround yourself with protectors — people who defend the culture, carry the values, and believe in the calling deeply.

Reflection Questions

1. Who strengthens my belief in the vision — and who weakens it?
2. What boundary needs to be set to protect momentum?

Author Quote — Coach David Angeron

"You can't build with people who secretly hope you lose."

July 30 — Leadership Isn't About Being Liked — It's About Being Effective

"If I were still trying to please people, I would not be a servant of Christ."
— Galatians 1:10

If your highest goal is to be liked, leadership will crush you. You'll soften truth, avoid hard conversations, delay necessary decisions, and compromise standards — all to keep people happy. But leadership is not popularity management; it's assignment management.

Effective leaders care more about obedience to God than approval from people. They still lead with love, humility, and compassion, but they refuse to trade effectiveness for applause. Sometimes the decisions that serve the mission best will make some people uncomfortable, confused, or even upset.

Being liked is temporary. Being effective leaves a legacy that impacts lives for years. At the end of your life, you won't answer to public opinion — you'll answer to God. Lead in a way that Heaven applauds, even if Earth doesn't always understand.

Reflection Questions

1. Am I prioritizing approval or effectiveness?
2. What decision would I make if rejection didn't scare me?

Author Quote — Coach David Angeron

"Being liked is temporary — being effective leaves a legacy."

July 31 — The Leader's Reward Is Impact, Not Applause

Applause fades. Awards collect dust. Public recognition comes and goes with seasons and trends. But impact — the lives changed, the leaders developed, the families strengthened, the culture transformed — that's the real reward of leadership.

You were not called to chase claps; you were called to hear one sentence from Jesus: "Well done." Some of your most impactful leadership moments will happen in private: a conversation no one hears about, a sacrifice no one sees, a decision no one celebrates but Heaven does.

When purpose becomes your motivation, criticism loses power and praise loses control. You stay steady, knowing God is keeping score in ways the world never will. Let eternity define success, not social approval. Impact outlives applause every time.

Reflection Questions

1. What motivates me more — praise or purpose?
2. Who has been impacted by my leadership that I can celebrate today?

Author Quote — Coach David Angeron

"The loudest praise you'll ever hear is from God — not the crowd."

✝

AUGUST

WORK ETHIC, DRIVE & PERSONAL STANDARDS

August 1 — People Are Your Greatest Asset

Organizations don't grow — people do. Strategies, systems, and structures matter, but they only go as far as the people who carry them. When people grow, everything grows: performance, creativity, loyalty, and impact. When people are neglected, eventually everything cracks — no matter how impressive the plan looks on paper.

As a leader, your greatest investment is not in buildings, branding, or budgets — it's in the hearts and minds of the people God has entrusted to you. Their emotional health, sense of belonging, spiritual life, and clarity of purpose will do more for your mission than the most polished playbook ever could.

When you encourage, coach, mentor, and develop people, they don't just execute tasks — they take ownership of the mission. Developed people think better, serve better, and lead better. Treat them like tools, and they'll eventually burn out. Treat them like treasures, and they'll multiply what's in your hands.

Develop people, and they'll develop the mission.

Reflection Questions

1. Who on my team needs investment, encouragement, or development?

2. Am I treating people like tools for assignments — or treasures for the kingdom?

Author Quote — Coach David Angeron

"People will never go further for the mission than the leader is willing to go for them."

August 2 — Emotional Intelligence Creates Influence

People don't follow the smartest leaders — they follow the most emotionally aware ones. Intelligence may impress, but emotional intelligence builds trust. Emotional intelligence is the ability to understand what you feel, what others feel, and how those emotions affect decisions, communication, and culture.

A leader who can read the room, sense discouragement, recognize stress, and respond with wisdom will always carry more influence than a leader who only quotes data. EQ creates safety. When people feel safe, they tell the truth, bring their ideas, admit mistakes, and stay engaged. When they feel judged, dismissed, or misunderstood, they shut down.

Emotional intelligence doesn't mean you avoid hard conversations — it means you handle them with timing, empathy, and clarity. It means you manage your emotions instead of letting them manage you.

Understanding others multiplies influence, because people don't just remember what you decided — they remember how you made them feel in the process.

Reflection Questions

1. Do I listen to understand — or listen to respond?

2. What emotional habit could improve my relationships immediately?

Author Quote — Coach David Angeron

"Emotional intelligence builds influence faster than talent ever will."

AUGUST 3 — KINDNESS IS NOT WEAKNESS

"Clothe yourselves with compassion, kindness, humility." — Colossians 3:12

Strong leaders don't use authority to intimidate — they use influence to elevate. Kindness is not softness; it's strength under control. It's the choice to treat people with dignity, even when you're correcting them, challenging them, or holding them accountable.

Some leaders confuse harshness with toughness. They think that being demanding means being demeaning. But fear only produces short-term compliance — never long-term commitment. People will do the minimum for someone who intimidates them. They'll go the extra mile for someone who truly values them.

Kindness doesn't mean lowering standards. It means raising standards while preserving honor. It shows up in your tone, your timing, your willingness to listen, and your refusal to belittle. The more influence you have, the more your kindness (or lack of it) shapes the entire culture.

Kindness multiplies performance — fear only multiplies compliance. The strongest leaders are kind enough to tell the truth and strong enough to do it with grace.

Reflection Questions

1. Do people feel valued after interactions with me?

2. Who needs kindness from me — not criticism — right now?

Author Quote — Coach David Angeron

"Being kind doesn't make you soft — it makes you strong enough not to be hard."

August 4 — A Leader's Tone Becomes the Team's Atmosphere

Teams rarely rise above the emotional climate of the leader. Your words matter, but your *tone* often speaks first. When pressure hits, people instinctively watch the leader's face, posture, and response. If the leader is frantic, the team becomes anxious. If the leader is unpredictable, the team becomes fearful. If the leader is calm and composed, the team becomes confident and focused.

Your tone doesn't just affect communication — it trains your workplace. Over time, your reactions become the accepted "normal." If sarcasm, impatience, or anger define your tone, you'll see those same patterns ripple through meetings, emails, and conversations. But if you consistently respond with clarity, steadiness, and respect, you'll notice your team mirroring that same emotional maturity.

You can't always control the pressure around you, but you can control the atmosphere you bring into the room. Lead your own tone first — your team is already learning from it.

Reflection Questions

1. What tone do I bring to the room when pressure increases?

2. How can I communicate calm confidence even in stress?

Author Quote — Coach David Angeron

*"Leadership is not what you say —
it's the emotional temperature you bring into the room."*

August 5 — People Don't Quit Jobs — They Quit Leaders

"Carry each other's burdens." — Galatians 6:2

Most resignations are not about salary or workload — they're about leadership. People can endure hard days, heavy seasons, and demanding expectations when they feel valued and supported. But they struggle to stay where they feel unseen, unheard, or unappreciated.

People don't leave roles as often as they leave relationships. They leave environments where their opinions don't matter, their growth isn't encouraged, and their humanity is ignored. As a leader, you can't remove every challenge, but you *can* decide how people experience those challenges under your leadership.

Ask yourself: Do I care about who they are outside of what they produce? Do I notice when they're overloaded, discouraged, or quietly struggling? Do I celebrate growth, not just outcomes? Retention is not luck — it's leadership. When people feel safe, believed in, and supported, they don't just stay — they stay engaged.

A good paycheck keeps people employed — a good leader keeps them committed.

Reflection Questions

1. Do the people I lead feel valued beyond their productivity?

2. How can I show more support for the personal well-being of my team?

Author Quote — Coach David Angeron

"A good paycheck keeps people employed — a good leader keeps them committed."

August 6 — Trust Is Earned Through Consistency

"Let love and faithfulness never leave you." — Proverbs 3:3

Trust isn't earned in big moments — it's built in everyday patterns. People don't trust leaders because of one powerful meeting or one inspiring speech. They trust leaders who show up the same way, over and over again: steady, honest, fair, and predictable in character.

Unpredictable leaders create unstable environments. When people never know which version of you they'll get — calm or explosive, present or distracted, encouraging or critical — they stop fully opening up. They begin managing around your mood instead of working toward the mission.

Consistency doesn't mean perfection, but it does mean reliability. Do you keep your word? Do you follow through on what you say? Do you respond with emotional steadiness? Do you make decisions based on values, not just feelings? Over time, those patterns build or break trust.

Trust is not achieved by intensity — it is achieved by consistency.

Reflection Questions

1. What area of inconsistency might be weakening trust?

2. How can I show up this week with predictability and stability?

Author Quote — Coach David Angeron

"Trust is not achieved by intensity — it is achieved by consistency."

AUGUST 7 — LEADERS GO FIRST IN FORGIVENESS

"Forgive as the Lord forgave you." — Colossians 3:13

B itterness destroys teams faster than failure ever will. Failure can be learned from; bitterness quietly contaminates everything. Forgiveness is not pretending the offense never happened — it's choosing not to let it poison your heart or the culture.

Leaders set the tone. If a leader holds grudges, brings up old mistakes, or treats people based on their worst moments, the whole culture becomes guarded and defensive. People start hiding, blaming, and withdrawing instead of learning, owning, and growing.

Forgiveness doesn't mean there are no consequences or conversations. It means you address issues clearly, make decisions wisely — and then release the resentment. You refuse to replay the offense in your mind or use it as a weapon later.

Forgiveness restores momentum; resentment ruins it. When leaders go first in forgiveness, they model what it means to keep the mission bigger than personal offense.

Reflection Questions

1. Who have I emotionally forgiven — and who have I only mentally forgiven?

2. Do I need to apologize, release, or reconcile to restore peace?

Author Quote — Coach David Angeron

"Forgiveness isn't about who's right —
it's about keeping the mission bigger than the offense."

August 8 — Listening Is Leadership

People don't need a leader who always has something to say — they need a leader who makes space to hear them. Listening is not just being quiet; it's being fully present. It's putting the phone down, making eye contact, and leaning into what's really being said — and sometimes what isn't being said.

Listening communicates value. It tells people, "You matter. Your perspective matters. Your experience matters." When people feel truly heard, they trust more, contribute more, and stay more engaged. When they feel dismissed or constantly interrupted, they eventually disengage and silently pull back.

Wise leaders ask questions, invite ideas, and pay attention to emotions, not just words. They don't rush to fix or defend — they first seek to understand. That level of listening doesn't weaken authority; it strengthens it. When leaders listen to people, people listen to leaders.

Reflection Questions

1. Do I listen to understand or listen waiting for my turn to speak?

2. Who in my life or organization needs to feel heard this week?

Author Quote — Coach David Angeron

"When leaders listen to people, people listen to leaders."

AUGUST 9 — THE STRONGEST LEADERS STAY CALM IN STORMS

People watch the leader when things go wrong. They're not just listening to your words; they're studying your response. If you panic, they panic. If you spiral, they spiral. If you remain grounded, honest, and steady, they find strength in your stability.

Calm is not denial. It doesn't mean you ignore problems, sugarcoat reality, or avoid difficult decisions. Calm leadership acknowledges the challenge but refuses to be ruled by fear. It says, "Yes, this is serious — and we will face it with wisdom and confidence."

Your internal state becomes your external leadership. That's why your own spiritual, emotional, and mental health cannot be ignored. The more time you spend in God's presence, the more peace you'll carry into pressure-filled moments. The storm may rage around you — but it doesn't have to rage *within* you.

Reflection Questions

1. What recent situation exposed my level of emotional control?

2. How can I practice calm leadership when pressure rises?

Author Quote — Coach David Angeron

"Storms don't expose weakness — they reveal emotional strength."

August 10 — Accountability Is an Act of Love

"Speak the truth in love." — Ephesians 4:15

Accountability isn't punishment — it's protection. Holding people to high standards is one of the clearest ways to say, "I believe in your potential." Avoiding accountability may feel kind in the moment, but it ultimately allows people to stay stuck in patterns that will limit or even harm them.

Leaders who love their teams don't let them drift without correction. They step into hard conversations with clarity and compassion. They address issues early instead of waiting until damage is done. They separate identity from behavior: "I value you — and because I value you, I can't ignore this."

People may resist accountability at first, especially if they're not used to it. But over time, they come to respect leaders who are willing to tell them the truth in love. Accountability helps people become who they were called to be, not just who they are today.

Reflection Questions

1. Who needs accountability from me — not avoidance?

2. How can I correct people in a way that protects dignity?

Author Quote — Coach David Angeron

"Accountability isn't criticism — it is a commitment to someone's greatness."

August 11 — Don't Confuse Achievement With Emotional Health

A person can be hitting every goal and still be deeply hurting inside. Numbers can look great while someone's inner life is falling apart. Achievement is visible — emotional health is not. As a leader, you must remember that impressive performance doesn't always equal inner peace.

High performers often know how to push through pain, hide exhaustion, and keep producing. But unaddressed stress, anxiety, burnout, or personal struggles eventually surface — in health, relationships, or sudden decisions. Great leaders care about how people *are*, not just what they *do*.

Don't only ask, "Did you get it done?" Ask, "How are you really doing?" Make room for honest conversations, support, and rest. When people are emotionally healthy, they don't just perform better — they live better. And leadership isn't just about producing results; it's about stewarding people.

Reflection Questions

1. Have I ignored someone's struggle because their performance looks strong?

2. How can I check in on people — not just tasks?

Author Quote — Coach David Angeron

"Performance can hide wounds — presence can help heal them."

August 12 — Not Every Emotion Deserves a Reaction

Leadership requires emotional discipline. Feeling something is not the same as being led by it. Anger, frustration, fear, or disappointment may show up — but they don't get to drive. When leaders react impulsively, they say and do things that damage trust, culture, and credibility.

Self-control acts like a wall of protection. It doesn't block you from feeling; it blocks feelings from taking over. Instead of snapping back, you pause. Instead of sending the angry email, you wait. Instead of letting your mood lead the meeting, you choose your mindset before you walk in.

Emotions are real, but they are also temporary. Wise leaders learn to process them with God, with trusted people, and with healthy outlets — not with reckless words or decisions. Your influence grows when your reactions shrink.

Reflection Questions

1. What emotion tends to lead my reactions the most — and why?

2. What healthier emotional response can I practice this week?

Author Quote — Coach David Angeron

"Emotions are signals — not steering wheels."

August 13 — Healthy Relationships Fuel High Performance

The best teams don't just work well together — they *care* well for each other. High performance isn't built only on pressure, goals, and deadlines. It's built on trust, connection, and shared commitment.

When relationships are strong, feedback is easier to receive, conflict is easier to resolve, and collaboration is more natural. People don't just show up for a paycheck; they show up for each other and the mission. They push harder because they don't want to let the team down.

But when relationships are strained, even simple tasks feel heavy. Misunderstandings increase, defensiveness rises, and energy drains. That's why great leaders intentionally invest in relational health — not just operational efficiency.

Celebrate wins together. Learn together. Laugh together. Check in on one another as people, not just performers. Healthy relationships don't slow down performance — they sustain it.

Reflection Questions

1. What can I do to strengthen connection on my team?

2. Is there someone I need to appreciate before I expect performance?

Author Quote — Coach David Angeron

"People work harder for leaders who make them feel they belong."

AUGUST 14 — ASSUME POSITIVE INTENT

"Love always trusts." — 1 Corinthians 13:7

Misunderstandings often do more damage than actual mistakes. Many relational breakdowns don't start because someone was malicious — they start because motives were misinterpreted. When we assume the worst, we create distance, tension, and unnecessary conflict.

Assuming positive intent doesn't mean being naïve or ignoring patterns. It means choosing to believe, *unless clearly proven otherwise*, that people are trying, not attacking. It means you ask questions like, "Help me understand what you meant," instead of jumping to, "They don't care," or "They're against me."

Leaders who assume the worst create cultures of defensiveness. Leaders who assume the best create cultures of safety. Trust first, verify with conversation, and correct with clarity when needed. Love always leans toward trust before suspicion.

Reflection Questions

1. Have I attributed negative motives to someone without proof?
2. How can I communicate to clarify before I criticize?

Author Quote — Coach David Angeron

"Always think the best unless you're clearly shown the worst."

August 15 — Influence Is Earned Through Relationship

"Carry each other's burdens." — Galatians 6:2

Leadership authority doesn't come from a title — it comes from trust. You can have position without influence, but you cannot have influence without relationship. People may comply with a title, but they only open their hearts to someone they believe genuinely cares.

If you want people to follow you in difficult seasons, you must be present in ordinary seasons. Influence is built in hallway conversations, sincere check-ins, moments of encouragement, and times when you show up for people beyond what your job description requires.

Relational equity is like a bank account — every act of support, empathy, and presence makes a deposit. Correction, challenge, and high expectations are withdrawals. If you withdraw more than you deposit, eventually the account is empty.

You can coach people without connection — but you can't truly *influence* them. Influence is earned one relationship at a time.

Reflection Questions

1. Who have I been leading transactionally instead of relationally?

2. How can I deepen connection before giving direction?

Author Quote — Coach David Angeron

"You can coach people without connection — but you can't influence them."

August 16 — Encourage Publicly, Correct Privately

Praise builds confidence. Public criticism destroys trust. Correction is necessary — but dignity is essential. The way you handle someone's mistakes often matters more than the mistake itself. When leaders correct publicly, people don't just hear the words — they feel the embarrassment. It doesn't just damage performance; it damages identity.

Great leaders separate *behavior* from *worth*. They address issues in private, where the person can listen without shame and grow without an audience. Publicly, they look for opportunities to honor effort, progress, and wins. Over time, this creates a culture where people are not afraid to try, fail, and improve — because they know mistakes won't be used to humiliate them.

Honor in correction creates loyalty — embarrassment creates distance. When people know you will protect their dignity, they will trust your feedback and lean into your leadership.

Reflection Questions

1. Have I corrected anyone publicly when it could have been done privately?

2. How can my correction build someone up rather than tear them down?

Author Quote — Coach David Angeron

"Correction without dignity damages — correction with dignity develops."

August 17 — Leadership Is Service, Not Superiority

"Whoever wants to become great among you must be your servant."
— Matthew 20:26

Leadership isn't about being above people — it's about lifting people. The world often equates leadership with status, power, and privilege. But in the Kingdom, leadership is measured by how well you serve. Titles don't define leadership — service does. A leader may sit at the head of the table, but their calling is still to wash feet.

If leadership ever becomes self-serving, it's no longer leadership — it's ego management. Great leaders ask: *How can I make it easier for others to succeed? How can I remove barriers, provide clarity, and invest in their growth?*

Serving doesn't mean you're passive or weak. It means you use your strength, experience, and authority to benefit others, not just yourself. The more influence you gain, the more responsibility you carry to serve well.

If you're too big to serve, you're too small to lead.

Reflection Questions

1. Am I leading to elevate myself or to elevate others?

2. Who can I serve intentionally this week?

Author Quote — Coach David Angeron

"Leaders don't stand over people — they stand with them and for them."

August 18 — Don't Lead From Ego — Lead From Empathy

People follow leaders who understand them, not leaders who compete with them. Ego says, "Look at me." Empathy says, "I'm here for you." Ego creates distance — because people feel judged, compared, or dismissed. Empathy creates connection — because people feel seen, heard, and valued.

Empathy doesn't mean you agree with everything someone says or excuse poor behavior. It means you care enough to understand what they're feeling and why. Before you correct, you listen. Before you respond, you consider their perspective. When people feel emotionally safe, they perform courageously. When they feel emotionally attacked, they play small and hide.

Ego leads with pride and insecurity. Empathy leads with strength and humility. One pushes people away; the other pulls them closer. When you lead from empathy, you don't lose authority — you deepen it.

Reflection Questions

1. Do people feel understood when they speak to me — or evaluated?

2. Who can I intentionally give empathy rather than solutions today?

Author Quote — Coach David Angeron

"Ego looks down — empathy leans in."

August 19 — Your Team Doesn't Need a Perfect Leader — They Need an Honest One

"Each of you must put off falsehood and speak truthfully." — Ephesians 4:25

Leaders don't earn trust through perfection — they earn it through honesty. People don't expect you to have every answer or never feel pressure. What they expect is truth. Truth about challenges. Truth about direction. Truth about expectations.

When leaders pretend everything is fine, even when it's clearly not, teams feel the disconnect. They sense what isn't being said. Over time, that gap between reality and communication erodes trust. But when a leader says, "This is hard — but here's how we're going to approach it," confidence rises.

Honesty also applies to your own limitations. Saying, "I don't know yet, but I'm committed to finding out," is far more powerful than faking certainty. Transparency doesn't weaken your leadership — it humanizes it.

Honesty builds trust. Pretending destroys it.

Reflection Questions

1. Have I been avoiding vulnerability to protect my image?
2. Where could more transparency strengthen the team?

Author Quote — Coach David Angeron

"Perfection impresses people — honesty impacts them."

August 20 — Celebrate People Loudly and Often

"Encourage the disheartened." — 1 Thessalonians 5:14

People repeat what you celebrate. When you celebrate excellence, you'll see more excellence. When you celebrate growth, you'll see more growth. When you honor character, you'll see more integrity in the culture. Celebration is not a luxury — it's leadership.

Many leaders only speak up when something goes wrong. Over time, people start associating your voice with criticism, not encouragement. But when you intentionally point out what's right — effort, resilience, problem-solving, creativity, teamwork — you breathe energy into the culture.

Celebration doesn't always mean big awards or public ceremonies. Sometimes it's a text, a shoutout in a meeting, a handwritten note, or a simple, "I see how hard you're working — and it matters." That kind of recognition builds confidence, loyalty, and passion.

Correction changes behavior — celebration changes culture.

Reflection Questions

1. Who deserves celebration that I haven't acknowledged yet?

2. What milestone, progress, or growth can I highlight this week?

Author Quote — Coach David Angeron

"Correction changes behavior — celebration changes culture."

AUGUST 21 — DON'T TAKE THINGS PERSONALLY THAT AREN'T PERSONAL

"A person's wisdom yields patience." — Proverbs 19:11

Leadership requires a thick skin and a tender heart. If every frustrated comment, tense email, or disconnected response hits you personally, you'll lead from wounds instead of wisdom. Often, people are not reacting *to you* — they're reacting to stress, fear, insecurity, or pressure in their own life. You just happen to be nearby.

Wise leaders pause before they personalize. They ask, "Is this truly about me — or is this about what they're going through?" That simple question can prevent unnecessary offense and emotional overreaction.

Not taking things personally doesn't mean you ignore disrespect or avoid boundaries. It means you respond thoughtfully instead of internalizing everything as an attack. When you stop absorbing every reaction as rejection, you gain the emotional freedom to lead clearly, calmly, and compassionately.

Reflection Questions

1. What recent situation did I internalize emotionally instead of assessing logically?

2. How can I respond without absorbing others' emotional state?

Author Quote — Coach David Angeron

"Leaders can't lead well if they're wounded by every word."

August 22 — Know the Difference Between Difficult People and Hurting People

Not everyone who frustrates you is difficult — some are hurting. There's a difference between someone who is toxic and someone who is wounded. Sometimes, the behavior that bothers you is a symptom of a battle you don't see: grief, insecurity, fear, exhaustion, or personal crisis.

Leaders with emotional intelligence respond with discernment, not assumption. They ask, "Is this defiance — or is this pain?" Compassion doesn't excuse unhealthy behavior, but it helps you address it with wisdom. Instead of immediately pushing someone away, you might need to pull them aside and say, "Are you okay? This doesn't seem like you."

Some people absolutely need boundaries and correction. Others need a safe place to heal so they can return to strength. Great leaders don't just manage performance — they care for people.

Reflection Questions

1. Have I labeled someone "difficult" instead of seeking to understand them?

2. What hurting person might need patience rather than rejection?

Author Quote — Coach David Angeron

"Some people don't need discipline — they need healing."

AUGUST 23 — DELIVER FEEDBACK WITH CLARITY, NOT CONDEMNATION

Feedback is essential for growth — but the way you deliver it determines whether it builds or breaks. People don't fear feedback; they fear humiliation, shame, or vague criticism that leaves them confused and discouraged.

Healthy feedback is clear, specific, and focused on behavior, not identity. Instead of "You're not doing a good job," say, "Here's what needs to change, and here's how I believe you can improve." Grace and truth can live in the same sentence: "I believe in you — and because I do, I need to challenge you on this."

Condemnation attacks the person; clarity addresses the problem. One leaves people feeling small. The other inspires them to grow. Feedback should sharpen people, not shatter them.

Reflection Questions

1. Does my correction leave people defeated or motivated?

2. What phrase or approach can make feedback more constructive and encouraging?

Author Quote — Coach David Angeron

"Feedback should sharpen people — not shatter them."

August 24 — Leaders Notice the Person Others Overlook

"The last will be first." — Matthew 20:16

Some of the greatest potential in your organization is hidden in people who aren't loud, flashy, or confident. They may not draw attention in meetings, but they serve faithfully, think deeply, and carry untapped gifts. Great leaders don't just notice the obvious stars — they scan the room for the overlooked.

Jesus consistently elevated the people others walked past — the unnoticed, the underestimated, the ones in the background. When you stop only valuing the most visible and start seeing the most faithful, you unlock a different level of impact.

A small word of belief can awaken massive calling. "I see how consistent you are." "I noticed the detail you put into that." "You have leadership in you." Those words can change how someone sees themselves.

Spot potential — and speak to it.

Reflection Questions

1. Who on my team is unseen or undervalued despite effort?

2. How can I elevate or encourage someone who rarely gets attention?

Author Quote — Coach David Angeron

"What you notice in people becomes what they begin to see in themselves."

August 25 — Don't Let One Person Poison the Whole Culture

Negativity is contagious — but so is positivity. It only takes one person consistently spreading cynicism, gossip, blame, or division to weaken the enthusiasm of an entire team. Culture rarely collapses from one big blow; it erodes slowly through small tolerances.

Leaders must be courageous enough to confront culture threats early. That might mean a direct conversation about attitude, a reset of expectations, or, in some cases, releasing someone who refuses to align. Hoping it will "just go away" is not leadership — it's avoidance.

Your responsibility is not just to the one person; it's to the entire team and mission. Protecting culture sometimes means making uncomfortable decisions. You can't build a winning environment while allowing poison to sit in the center of it.

Reflection Questions

1. Have I allowed a negative influence to continue unchecked?

2. Do I need to coach, correct, or remove someone to protect unity?

Author Quote — Coach David Angeron

"Culture doesn't fail from one big problem — but from many small tolerances."

AUGUST 26 — PEOPLE DON'T NEED PERFECTION — THEY NEED PRESENCE

When someone is struggling, you don't need a perfect speech — you just need to show up. Many leaders stay silent because they're unsure what to say, so they say nothing at all. But presence often matters more than words. A text, a call, a quick check-in, or simply sitting with someone can speak louder than the most polished advice.

Presence says, "You're not alone." It communicates value, comfort, and solidarity: "I don't have all the answers, but I'm here with you in it." That's the heart of pastoral leadership in the workplace — not just managing performance, but standing with people in pain.

Support is not always spoken — sometimes it's shown. People remember who stood with them in their hardest seasons far more than who praised them in their best ones.

Reflection Questions

1. Who is hurting, stressed, or discouraged that I can simply be there for?

2. Do I rush to solve things instead of showing support?

Author Quote — Coach David Angeron

"Presence heals places where advice never reaches."

AUGUST 27 — LEADERS SPEAK LIFE

"The tongue has the power of life and death." — Proverbs 18:21

Words don't cost anything — but they change everything. A single sentence can plant courage or plant doubt. The right word at the right time can shift someone's mindset, restore their confidence, and remind them of who they are in Christ and in their calling.

Leaders must be intentional with their language. Don't just point out what's broken; point out what's building. Don't only speak to current performance; speak to future potential. Life-giving leaders say things like, "I believe in you," "You're growing," "You're called to this," and "You have more in you than you realize."

Speaking life doesn't mean ignoring problems. It means framing them with hope, identity, and faith. Your words are seeds — and culture is the soil. Over time, whatever you consistently speak will begin to grow.

Reflection Questions

1. Who needs life spoken into them this week?

2. What positive truth can I affirm publicly or privately?

Author Quote — Coach David Angeron

"Your words are seeds — plant what you want to grow."

AUGUST 28 — DON'T EXPECT WHAT YOU AREN'T WILLING TO MODEL

"Set an example for the believers in speech, in conduct, in love, in faith and in purity." — 1 Timothy 4:12

People don't follow instructions — they follow examples. If you expect excellence, but give halfway effort, your words will ring hollow. If you demand integrity, but cut corners yourself, your credibility disappears. Culture is not what you *say*; it's what you *show*.

You reproduce what you demonstrate. If you model humility, teachability, and hard work, your team is far more likely to embody those traits. If you model gossip, inconsistency, or unchecked emotion, don't be surprised when those habits appear in the culture.

Leadership means going first in the behavior you want to see. It doesn't mean perfection, but it does mean ownership: "I'm asking you to do what I'm striving to live myself." That level of alignment builds respect and trust.

Reflection Questions

1. Where might I be expecting from others what I'm not consistently modeling?

2. What personal behavior shift would positively influence my team?

Author Quote — Coach David Angeron

"Your example is louder than your expectations."

AUGUST 29 — LEADERSHIP REQUIRES EMOTIONAL MARGIN

"Be still, and know that I am God." — Psalm 46:10

If you are constantly overwhelmed, everything will feel like a crisis. Emotional margin is the space between your limits and your load. Without it, patience runs out, clarity fades, and small problems feel like massive threats. The result? Overreactions, poor decisions, and strained relationships.

Leadership requires intentional rest — not just physical, but emotional and spiritual. Time in God's presence, unplugged moments, healthy relationships, and rhythms of rest all refill what leadership drains. Emotional margin doesn't mean you avoid responsibility; it means you protect your ability to carry it well.

When you lead from exhaustion, you react. When you lead from overflow, you respond with wisdom. Rest is not selfish — it's a leadership responsibility.

Reflection Questions

1. Am I leading from overflow or exhaustion?
2. Where can I build space in my schedule to protect emotional margin?

Author Quote — Coach David Angeron

"Exhausted leaders don't make wise decisions."

August 30 — Stop Expecting Everyone to Think Like You

Just because someone thinks differently doesn't mean they're wrong — it means they're different. God designed teams with diverse perspectives, personalities, and problem-solving styles for a reason. Strong leaders don't demand clones; they cultivate collaboration.

If everyone thinks like you, the team only has one brain. You may feel validated, but you won't be stretched. Growth happens when you're willing to hear ideas that challenge your assumptions and expand your vision.

Different doesn't equal disloyal. Sometimes the people who see things differently are the very ones God placed in your life to protect you from blind spots. Your job is not to shut them down, but to listen with curiosity, filter with wisdom, and decide with clarity.

Reflection Questions

1. Do I listen to alternative ideas with curiosity or defensiveness?

2. How can I create more space for different perspectives?

Author Quote — Coach David Angeron

"If everyone thinks like you, the team only has one brain."

AUGUST 31 — A LEADER'S GREATEST SKILL IS EMOTIONAL SELF-CONTROL

"A gentle answer turns away wrath." — Proverbs 15:1

Technical skills matter. Strategy matters. Experience matters. But emotional self-control is what sustains leadership over time. Your ability to stay steady when others are reactive, to respond kindly when attacked, and to stay grounded when pressure rises is one of your greatest advantages.

Without self-control, talent becomes dangerous. Your words hit harder, your reactions cut deeper, and your decisions become less wise. With self-control, your presence calms the room, your words carry more weight, and your leadership becomes trustworthy.

Emotional control is not pretending you don't feel — it's mastering how you express what you feel. It's taking emotions to God before taking them out on people. A leader who can control their emotions can often change the atmosphere with a single response.

Reflection Questions

1. Do my reactions under pressure build trust or damage it?

2. What triggers do I need to master instead of excuse?

Author Quote — Coach David Angeron

"A leader who can control their emotions can control their environment."

SEPTEMBER

COMMUNICATION,
INFLUENCE & IMPACT

September 1 — Strength Begins With Stillness

"In quietness and trust is your strength." — Isaiah 30:15

The world tells leaders to push harder. God tells leaders to rest deeper. Culture shouts, "Hustle more. Do more. Prove more." But heaven whispers, "Be still, and know that I am God." Stillness is not laziness — it's alignment. It is the intentional choice to pause your pace so God can realign your heart.

In stillness, God recalibrates your motives, restores your peace, and refocuses your priorities. You're not just stepping away from noise; you're stepping closer to Him. True strength doesn't come from constant motion — it comes from constant connection. When you build your schedule but neglect His presence, you build pressure without power.

You don't recharge by withdrawing from responsibility — you recharge by drawing near to God in the middle of it. The leader who learns to pause in God's presence will stand stronger in people's pressure.

Reflection Questions

1. Do I rest with God or simply rest from work?

2. Where can I make space for stillness this week?

Author Quote — Coach David Angeron

"Strength doesn't flow from movement — it flows from connection."

September 2 — You Can Be Busy and Spiritually Empty

"What good is it… if he forfeits his soul?" — Mark 8:36

You can be applauded publicly and empty privately. You can fill your calendar and starve your spirit. Busyness is often praised in leadership, but heaven is not impressed by overloaded schedules and undernourished souls. The most dangerous version of a leader is not the inexperienced one — it's the spiritually empty one.

You can do ministry and neglect your soul. You can grow a business and shrink spiritually. Activity is not intimacy. Just because you're working *for* God doesn't mean you're walking *with* God. Eventually, emptiness leaks — into your decisions, your tone, your relationships, and your perspective.

Spiritual health doesn't happen accidentally; it requires intentional time in God's Word, prayer, worship, and honest reflection. Your soul is not an accessory to your leadership — it's the engine. If the engine is dry, nothing runs right.

You can't pour into others if you're spiritually dehydrated.

Reflection Questions

1. Have I confused productivity with spiritual health?

2. What practice helps restore my soul that I've neglected?

Author Quote — Coach David Angeron

"A dry leader can't refresh anyone."

September 3 — Rest Is a Weapon

"He makes me lie down in green pastures." — Psalm 23:2

Rest is not laziness — it is spiritual strength. The enemy knows that a tired leader is a vulnerable leader. Exhaustion weakens discernment, shortens your patience, blurs your vision, and amplifies your emotions. That's why spiritual attack often intensifies when you're worn down.

Rest is not God's suggestion — it's His design. He "makes" you lie down because He knows you won't choose it naturally. Rest sharpens your thinking, softens your heart, and restores your sensitivity to God's voice. It doesn't mean you abandon responsibility; it means you return to it refueled.

Sometimes the most spiritual thing you can do is rest — sleep, unplug, breathe, worship, be present with God and the people you love. Rest doesn't mean you stop caring about the mission; it means you care enough to protect the leader who carries it.

Reflection Questions

1. Do I treat rest as a necessity or a reward?
2. Where is fatigue affecting my decision-making or attitude?

Author Quote — Coach David Angeron

"Leaders don't break from pressure — they break from neglecting rest."

September 4 — Protect Your Peace Like It's a Priority

"Let the peace of Christ rule in your hearts." — Colossians 3:15

Peace is not passive — it is something you must guard. The peace of Christ is meant to *rule* your heart, not visit it occasionally. Anything that constantly disrupts your peace will eventually disrupt your purpose.

You cannot lead clearly if your mind is noisy with drama, negativity, fear, and constant chaos. Your peace is a spiritual asset — and the enemy targets it through toxic relationships, unnecessary conflicts, overcommitment, and constant comparison. It's not selfish to protect your peace — it's strategic.

Sometimes guarding your peace means saying no to certain conversations, limiting certain influences, or setting boundaries that feel uncomfortable but necessary. The leader who protects their peace leads with clarity, calm, and conviction. The leader who neglects it leads from reaction and reactivity.

If peace is stolen, strength is stolen.

Reflection Questions

1. What consistently disrupts my peace — and why do I allow it?

2. What boundary will help protect my emotional and spiritual well-being?

Author Quote — Coach David Angeron

"Peace is not a place you escape to — it's a mindset you protect."

September 5 — Burnout Is Not a Badge of Honor

Burnout is not proof of dedication — it is proof of misalignment. Heaven is not applauding your exhaustion. You were never meant to carry every burden, fix every problem, or say yes to every need. When you take on assignments God didn't give you, you take on weights He never promised to lift.

There is a difference between being poured out and being completely drained. God's calling comes with God's strength. When you are constantly operating beyond grace and within ego, you begin to live in strain instead of surrender.

Jesus invites you to His yoke — His pace, His priorities, His rhythm of work and rest. That doesn't mean the path is easy, but it means you're not crushed by it. If the assignment is slowly destroying your joy, health, or family, it's time to evaluate whether it's God's assignment or people's expectations.

Reflection Questions

1. Am I busy with what God called me to — or what people pressured me into?

2. What responsibilities do I need to release rather than cling to?

Author Quote — Coach David Angeron

"If the load is crushing you, it's not God's load."

September 6 — You Can't Heal When You Refuse to Slow Down

"He restores my soul." — Psalm 23:3

Some leaders move so fast that they outrun their healing. They push past disappointment, betrayal, stress, and grief by staying busy — but pain buried alive is pain that resurfaces later. Unaddressed hurt will eventually leak into your leadership: your tone gets sharper, your trust gets smaller, your patience gets shorter.

Healing requires reflection, honesty, and rest. It requires you to slow down long enough to feel what you've been avoiding and bring it to God. Restoration doesn't happen while you're sprinting from meeting to meeting and crisis to crisis. It happens in quiet moments where you allow God to touch what hustle can't fix.

God can restore what you're willing to rest. When you stop numbing with busyness and start inviting Him into the wound, healing begins. A whole leader is far more powerful than a hurried one.

Reflection Questions

1. Am I using busyness to escape what needs healing?

2. What wound needs attention and restoration with God?

Author Quote — Coach David Angeron

"Rest isn't where healing ends — it's where healing begins."

September 7 — Mental Strength Begins With What You Feed Your Mind

Your mind is a battleground, and whatever you feed it will grow. You cannot live in constant negativity and expect to think with faith. You cannot binge fear-filled news, toxic content, or comparison-driven social media and expect to walk in confidence.

Negativity breeds fear. Worry breeds anxiety. Scripture breeds faith. Gratitude breeds joy. Leaders must become gatekeepers of their thoughts — filtering what enters, what stays, and what must be rejected. Renewing your mind is not a one-time event; it is a daily discipline.

Filling your mind with God's Word, worship, truth, and healthy perspectives is not optional if you want emotional and spiritual resilience. Your inner narrative becomes your outer reality.

If you want a stronger mind, give it stronger fuel.

Reflection Questions

1. What mental content have I been consuming that weakens me?
2. What truth from God's Word do I need to meditate on daily?

Author Quote — Coach David Angeron

"Whatever dominates your mind eventually directs your life."

September 8 — Stop Carrying Burdens That Belong to God

"Cast all your anxieties on Him because He cares for you." — 1 Peter 5:7

You weren't designed to carry everything alone. Leadership can trick you into believing that if you don't hold it all together, everything will fall apart. That pressure creates silent panic. But worry doesn't remove weight — it multiplies it.

Prayer doesn't ignore problems — it transfers ownership. Casting your cares on God is not pretending they don't exist; it's acknowledging you're not the best one to hold them. When you insist on controlling every outcome, you step into a role that was never yours. That's when your soul begins to collapse under pressure.

God cares for you — not just for your assignments, but for *you*. He invites you to lay burdens at His feet daily, not drag them around until you break.

Give God what only God can hold.

Reflection Questions

1. What burden have I been carrying instead of surrendering?

2. What would look different if I trusted God fully in this situation?

Author Quote — Coach David Angeron

"Peace begins where control ends."

September 9 — You Can't Do Everything — and You're Not Supposed To

"My grace is sufficient for you, for my power is made perfect in weakness."
— 2 Corinthians 12:9

Leaders often believe they must be strong everywhere, for everyone, all the time. That's not leadership — that's exhaustion. God never asked you to be limitless; He asked you to be dependent. He intentionally left weaknesses and gaps in your life so His strength could fill them.

Your need for God is not a flaw — it's design. When you pretend you can handle everything, you block the very grace that's trying to help you. Admitting, "I can't do this alone," is not failure — it's faith.

You are not called to be everyone's savior, fixer, or source. That role is already taken. You are called to be obedient, faithful, and surrendered.

Reflection Questions

1. Where have I placed unrealistic expectations on myself?

2. What weakness could be an invitation for God to work?

Author Quote — Coach David Angeron

"You were not called to be everything — you were called to be obedient."

September 10 —
Slow Down or Break Down

"Teach us to number our days, that we may gain a heart of wisdom."
— Psalm 90:12

When life moves too fast, you stop noticing what matters most: God's presence, people's hearts, and your own condition. Constant rushing leads to shallow thinking, impulsive decisions, and spiritual numbness. Slowing down isn't laziness — it's wisdom.

A life with no margin eventually collapses. Your body will signal it. Your emotions will show it. Your relationships will feel it. The warning signs are there long before the breakdown: irritability, constant fatigue, lack of joy, loss of focus, and spiritual dryness.

Slowing down means you intentionally create space — for God, for rest, for reflection, for real connection. Wisdom doesn't live in frantic motion; it lives in intentional pace.

Your soul needs pace, not pressure.

Reflection Questions

1. What warning signs of overload have I been ignoring?

2. Where can I intentionally reduce speed to increase awareness?

Author Quote — Coach David Angeron

"If you don't schedule rest, life will schedule collapse."

SEPTEMBER 11 —
YOUR THOUGHTS SHAPE YOUR REALITY

"As a man thinks in his heart, so is he." — Proverbs 23:7

Your life moves in the direction of your dominant thoughts. You cannot constantly think, *"I'm not enough, I'll never get through this, things never change,"* and then expect to live with courage, hope, and expectation. What you continually meditate on becomes what you eventually manifest.

You can't think defeat and live victorious. You can't think unworthy and walk confidently in your calling. You can't think small and lead big. The battlefield is often not around you but within you.

This is why renewing your mind with God's truth is essential. You don't just rebuke lies — you replace them. You actively choose to agree with what God says, even when your feelings lag behind. Over time, your internal narrative shifts, and your external life follows.

Winning begins in the mind before it appears in life.

Reflection Questions

1. What negative belief has shaped my decisions lately?
2. What truth from Scripture do I need to replace it with?

Author Quote — Coach David Angeron

"Your mindset will either be your ceiling or your superpower."

September 12 — Guard Your Mind From Future Fear

Most anxiety is not about what *is* happening — it's about what *might* happen. The enemy floods your imagination with worst-case scenarios to rob today's peace with tomorrow's fears. But worry is a thief — it charges you interest on outcomes that often never occur.

God is already in your tomorrow. He's not surprised by what's ahead. He goes before you, preparing provision, strength, wisdom, and favor. When you fixate on "What if?", you forget "Who is."

Guarding your mind from future fear doesn't mean ignoring responsibility or refusing to plan. It means planning with wisdom but trusting with faith. You do what you can — and trust God with what you can't.

You don't walk into the future alone — God walks ahead of you.

Reflection Questions

1. What future outcome am I fearing instead of trusting God with?

2. What past victory proves that God will come through again?

Author Quote — Coach David Angeron

"Worry imagines the worst — faith prepares for God's best."

September 13 —
Rest Allows Revelation

You hear God most clearly when life is quiet. Constant noise — notifications, deadlines, conversations, worries — drowns out the gentle leading of the Holy Spirit. Rest isn't just relief from pressure; it's a doorway to clarity.

There are answers, strategies, and ideas that God wants to reveal — but they're waiting on your attention, not your anxiety. Sometimes the breakthrough you're praying for doesn't come through more effort, but through deeper listening.

Still waters represent more than relaxation — they represent clarity, reflection, and direction. When you slow down, your spirit can finally catch up. You begin to sense God's nudges, hear His correction, and receive His reassurance.

Sometimes God stops the world around you to speak to the world within you.

Reflection Questions

1. Have I been listening to God or only talking to God?

2. What quiet space can I create for God to speak into my decisions?

Author Quote — Coach David Angeron

"If you want revelation, make space for silence."

September 14 —
Your Pace Impacts Your Peace

"Those who wait on the Lord shall renew their strength." — Isaiah 40:31

Rushing creates anxiety. Waiting on God creates clarity. When you move at culture's pace — faster, busier, louder — peace becomes scarce. When you move at God's pace — prayerful, intentional, surrendered — strength becomes renewable.

Not every open door is a God door. Not every opportunity is meant for *now*. Sometimes what looks like delay is actually divine protection from moving too soon or in the wrong direction.

Your pace is a spiritual decision. When you insist on your own timing, you inherit your own stress. When you surrender your timing to God, you inherit His peace.

Reflection Questions

1. Where am I rushing instead of trusting?
2. What would change if I moved at God's pace instead of culture's pace?

Author Quote — Coach David Angeron

"Peace isn't found in speed — it's found in surrender."

September 15 — You Don't Need More Strength — You Need More Surrender

"The Lord will fight for you; you need only be still." — Exodus 14:14

When battles intensify, our instinct is to fight harder, push more, and carry everything ourselves. But sometimes breakthrough doesn't come from increased effort — it comes from deeper surrender. God never asked you to be your own defender, provider, or rescuer.

When you fight in your own strength, you exhaust yourself. When you surrender the fight to God, you access His strength. Being still doesn't mean being passive; it means refusing to panic while God works on what you cannot.

Surrender sounds like, "God, I trust Your timing, Your strategy, and Your outcome more than my own." It's releasing control, not abandoning responsibility. You still show up — but you stop trying to be God.

Reflection Questions

1. What battle have I been trying to win in my own strength?

2. What would surrender look like in this situation?

Author Quote — Coach David Angeron

"Surrender isn't losing control — it's trusting the One who actually has it."

September 16 — Your Soul Needs More Than Success

"Man shall not live on bread alone, but on every word that comes from the mouth of God." — Matthew 4:4

You can hit every earthly goal and still feel empty inside. Success can grow your platform while quietly shrinking your soul if you're not careful. You can build a recognizable brand and lose your joy. You can hit financial milestones and lose your peace. When your metrics rise but your spiritual life declines, that's not winning — that's warning.

Your soul was never designed to be satisfied by numbers, titles, or applause. It was designed to be filled by God's presence, God's Word, and God's voice. Business, leadership, and influence are assignments — not identities. When you attach your worth to what you're building instead of Who is building you, anxiety and insecurity creep in.

Feed your spirit intentionally: time in Scripture, worship, silence with God, honest prayer, and gratitude. Success is a gift — but it is a terrible substitute for spiritual intimacy.

Reflection Questions

1. Have I been feeding my success more than my spirit?

2. What can I do this week to nourish my soul intentionally?

Author Quote — Coach David Angeron

"Never sacrifice your soul on the altar of success."

September 17 — Discipline Restores What Emotion Destroys

"The spirit is willing, but the flesh is weak." — Matthew 26:41

Your emotions don't always want what's good for you. They want relief, not refinement. They chase comfort, shortcuts, and escape. One bad day, one harsh comment, or one disappointing result can cause your emotions to say, "Quit. Drift. Numb out." That's where discipline steps in.

Discipline protects your future from your feelings. It keeps you anchored when motivation fades and emotions fluctuate. You don't have to feel motivated to be consistent — you just have to be committed to the habits that honor your calling.

Daily disciplines — prayer, planning, healthy routines, exercise, time in the Word, focused work — rebuild what emotional reactions often tear down. Discipline creates structure when your feelings create chaos. It gives you a path to follow when your mood offers you an exit.

Emotions are real, but they are not reliable leaders. Discipline builds a life emotions can't sabotage.

Reflection Questions

1. Where have emotions taken the lead over discipline?
2. What daily routine helps restore structure and strength in my life?

Author Quote — Coach David Angeron

"Emotions crave comfort — discipline creates freedom."

September 18 — What You Refuse to Process Will Eventually Control You

Unprocessed pain becomes internal pressure. You can bury it with busyness, hide it behind performance, or ignore it with distraction, but it doesn't disappear — it waits. The emotions you refuse to acknowledge start leaking into your tone, your decisions, your relationships, and your leadership.

Anger turns into harshness. Disappointment turns into cynicism. Fear turns into control. Often it's not the current situation making you react so strongly — it's the old wound you never processed.

Healing begins with honesty, not hiding. God already sees your anxiety, your grief, your disappointment, and your fear. He's not waiting for you to "get over it"; He's waiting for you to bring it. Inviting God into your pain — through prayer, journaling, counseling, or honest conversation — opens the door to freedom.

Repressed emotions don't disappear — they accumulate. Confronting them is not weakness; it's wisdom.

Reflection Questions

1. What emotion have I been suppressing instead of surrendering?

2. When will I give myself permission to feel and heal?

Author Quote — Coach David Angeron

"You can't conquer what you won't confront."

September 19 —
You Can Start Over Anytime

"His mercies are new every morning." — Lamentations 3:23

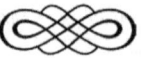

The enemy loves to whisper, "You blew it. It's too late. You missed your chance." But grace says, "Begin again." As long as you are breathing, you are not beyond God's ability to restore, redirect, or redeem.

You haven't missed your moment. You haven't ruined God's plan. You may have taken detours, made poor decisions, or stalled in fear — but God's mercy is stronger than your missteps. Every sunrise is heaven's declaration that yesterday's failures don't have to define today's choices.

Starting over doesn't always mean changing careers, cities, or roles. Sometimes starting over means a fresh mindset, a renewed commitment, a humbled heart, or a new habit.

The enemy reminds you of your failure; God reminds you of your future. Don't stay stuck in shame when grace has already opened a new door. Every day is a reset button — use it.

Reflection Questions

1. What part of my life needs a fresh start instead of shame?
2. What step will I take today to restart momentum?

Author Quote — Coach David Angeron

"If you woke up today, God is not done — and neither are you."

September 20 — Your Thoughts Need Boundaries Too

"Take captive every thought." — 2 Corinthians 10:5

Just because a thought arrives doesn't mean it deserves residence. The enemy rarely attacks only through circumstances — he attacks through suggestion. Thoughts like *"You're not enough... You'll always fail... No one cares... It's too late..."* are not harmless; they are spiritual strategies.

Thoughts become beliefs when you agree with them. A passing doubt becomes a prison when you give it permission to stay. That's why Scripture calls you to *take captive every thought* — to test it, confront it, and replace it if it doesn't align with God's truth.

You are not a helpless victim to your thoughts — you are the guardian of your mind. Set boundaries: what you will meditate on, what you will reject, and what you will replace. When you let God's Word be the filter, lies lose their power.

Reflection Questions

1. What thoughts have been allowed access that should have been rejected?

2. What truth can replace the lie I've been battling?

Author Quote — Coach David Angeron

"A thought becomes a prison the moment you agree with it."

September 21 — Mental Strength Grows Through Consistency, Not Intensity

You don't become mentally strong from one powerful moment — you become strong from many faithful ones. A single great day of discipline doesn't transform your mindset; a pattern of discipline does. Emotional and mental health aren't built in emotional highs but in daily habits.

Small, steady steps beat occasional big efforts. Reading a chapter of Scripture daily transforms more than reading an entire book once a month. Taking a short walk consistently does more than one intense workout followed by weeks of inactivity. Practicing gratitude each day builds more joy than a rare moment of inspiration.

We often wait for a burst of motivation to change, but transformation comes from repeated practices, not random passions. Consistency builds resilience, clarity, and confidence. When you keep showing up, even when you don't feel like it, mental strength quietly multiplies.

Reflection Questions

1. Where have I relied on bursts of motivation instead of building habits?

2. What one consistent practice would strengthen my mental health?

Author Quote — Coach David Angeron

"Transformation doesn't come from occasional passion — but repeated practices."

September 22 — Protect Your Mind From Comparison

"Let each one examine his own work." — Galatians 6:4

Comparison is mental poison. It turns another person's progress into your perceived failure. It turns someone else's blessing into your internal criticism. God didn't design comparison to be a measuring stick — He designed *calling* to be.

The race God gave you doesn't look like anyone else's. Different seasons. Different battles. Different timing. When you constantly measure yourself against others, you stop noticing what God is actually doing in you. Gratitude fades, joy dims, and contentment disappears.

Celebrating others is healthy; comparing yourself to them is harmful. You can cheer for someone's win without questioning your worth. Your assignment is not to outpace them — it's to be faithful where you are.

Focus on progress, not comparison. Ask, "Am I growing from who I was?" instead of "Am I matching who they are?"

Reflection Questions

1. What area of my life is most affected by comparison?

2. How can I focus on progress rather than comparison?

Author Quote — Coach David Angeron

"Comparison blinds you to everything God is building in you."

September 23 — God Does His Best Work in Broken Places

"My power is made perfect in weakness." — 2 Corinthians 12:9

God doesn't wait until you're fully healed to use you — He uses you while He heals you. Your weakness is not a disqualification; it's an opportunity for His strength to be displayed. The places you feel most fragile can become the places He shines most brightly.

We often hide our brokenness, thinking that leadership requires flawless strength and polished stories. But Scripture is filled with leaders whose greatest impact came through their greatest weakness — Moses' insecurity, David's failure, Paul's thorn. God doesn't showcase perfect people; He showcases perfect grace.

That painful part of your story — the loss, the setback, the struggle — may become the exact place God uses to reach others. Your story becomes strongest where you once struggled the most, because His faithfulness is most obvious there.

You are not powerful because you're flawless — you're powerful because He's faithful.

Reflection Questions

1. What broken place have I been hiding rather than offering to God?

2. How has God already used pain in my story to help others?

Author Quote — Coach David Angeron

"God doesn't need your perfection — He needs your permission."

September 24 —
Strong Leaders Ask for Help

"Two are better than one." — Ecclesiastes 4:9

Independence sounds strong, but isolation is weak. The belief that "I have to handle everything alone" doesn't make you a hero — it makes you a target. When leaders refuse support, stress multiplies and perspective shrinks. When they receive help, strength multiplies and clarity returns.

Even Moses needed Aaron to speak for him. Even David needed Jonathan to encourage him. Even Jesus chose disciples to walk beside Him. If the Son of God didn't lead alone, neither should you.

Asking for help isn't an admission of failure — it's an act of wisdom and humility. It might look like asking for prayer, delegating a task, seeking counsel, or being honest about your limits. Strength is not proven by carrying everything; it's proven by building a team around what God has called you to do.

Reflection Questions

1. What support have I been avoiding because of pride or fear?

2. Who can I reach out to for help, accountability, or encouragement?

Author Quote — Coach David Angeron

"Asking for help doesn't make you less of a leader — it makes you a lasting one."

SEPTEMBER 25 — YOU WILL NEVER LOSE WHAT YOU GIVE TO GOD

"Commit to the Lord whatever you do, and He will establish your plans."
— Proverbs 16:3

Anything you surrender to God becomes safe. Anything you refuse to surrender becomes vulnerable. When you clutch your plans, relationships, resources, or dreams with a tight grip, fear grows — *What if I lose this? What if it fails?* But when you place them in God's hands, peace grows — because He is responsible for what He holds.

God cannot fully bless what you insist on controlling. Control keeps you in charge, but it also keeps you limited. Surrender invites His wisdom, His timing, and His provision into the areas you care about most.

You don't risk losing when you surrender to God — you risk losing when you don't. What you entrust to Him may change shape, timing, or expression, but it will always be handled with purpose.

Reflection Questions

1. What area of my life am I afraid to fully surrender?

2. What is God asking me to trust Him with right now?

Author Quote — Coach David Angeron

"What you surrender to God doesn't decrease — it increases."

September 26 — Rest Isn't an Escape — It's a Strategy

"In all your ways acknowledge Him, and He will make your paths straight."
— Proverbs 3:6

Rest doesn't take you off mission — it prepares you for it. Many leaders treat rest like an escape: collapse on the couch, zone out, scroll endlessly. That kind of "rest" numbs you but doesn't restore you. True rest is strategic — it's intentional time to refocus, reflect, breathe, pray, and realign with God.

When you acknowledge God in your rhythm, not just your responsibilities, He straightens your path and sharpens your perspective. Rest gives you space to evaluate: What's working? What isn't? What needs to change? Where is God leading next?

Rest is not wasted time; it's preparation time. You're either recharging or you're quietly draining. Strategic rest makes you sharper in decision-making, healthier in relationships, and more stable under pressure.

Reflection Questions

1. Is my rest intentional or accidental?

2. What practice can help me experience peaceful, purposeful rest this week?

Author Quote — Coach David Angeron

"Rest doesn't take you off mission — it restores you for the mission."

September 27 — God Renews What You Release

G od cannot renew what you insist on carrying alone. Many leaders grit their teeth, push through, and hold everything together on the outside while quietly collapsing on the inside. But Jesus doesn't say, "Manage your burden better." He says, "Bring it to Me."

Strength isn't found in pretending you're fine — it's found in coming to Him weary and honest. When you release fear, He restores peace. When you release worry, He restores confidence. When you release control, He restores clarity.

Surrender is not giving up; it's giving over. It is the conscious decision to say, "God, I can't carry this anymore, but I believe You can." Breakthrough often begins at the moment of release, not at the moment of effort.

Reflection Questions

1. What am I holding that God is asking me to release?

2. How would my peace change if I fully trusted God in this situation?

Author Quote — Coach David Angeron

"Your load gets lighter the moment you decide it no longer belongs to you."

September 28 — A Healthy Mind Requires a Healthy Environment

You cannot maintain a healthy mind while staying in consistently unhealthy environments. If your surroundings are filled with constant complaining, gossip, negativity, fear, or drama, your thoughts will eventually mirror that noise. Environment is not neutral — it is shaping you.

Peace requires boundaries. Growth requires separation. Sometimes you need distance — not because you're better than others, but because you're responsible for what God has placed in you. The voices around you either feed your faith or fuel your fear.

A healthy environment doesn't mean everything is perfect; it means there is honesty, encouragement, accountability, and hope. Choose wisely where you spend your time, who you spend it with, and what atmospheres you continually expose yourself to.

Your environment affects your emotions — and your emotions affect your decisions.

Reflection Questions

1. Who or what consistently drains my peace?
2. What boundary can I set to protect my mental health?

Author Quote — Coach David Angeron

"Your environment is either feeding your focus or fighting it."

September 29 — God Is Not Asking You to Be Strong — He's Asking You to Be Still

The world trains leaders to power through. God trains leaders to pause. We often believe that if we stop pushing, everything will fall apart. But God says, "Be still, and *know* that I am God" — not "Be busy and prove that you are enough."

Strength is not always proven by nonstop motion. Sometimes it's proven by trusting stillness — by choosing to pause, breathe, and remember Who is actually in control. Stillness is not laziness; it's surrender. It's stepping back internally and saying, "God, I recognize that You are God — I am not."

When you stop striving and start trusting, God steps in. Stillness invites supernatural strength, wisdom, and perspective into situations your hustle can't fix.

Reflection Questions

1. Where am I striving for control instead of trusting God?
2. How can I make space for stillness this week?

Author Quote — Coach David Angeron

"God can do more with your stillness than you can do with your struggle."

September 30 —
Protect Your Mental Strength the Way Athletes Protect Their Body

"Above all else, guard your heart." — Proverbs 4:23

Athletes stretch, fuel, hydrate, train, and recover because they know performance depends on preparation. They understand that neglect leads to injury. Leaders must treat their minds the same way. Mental strength doesn't appear randomly — it's developed intentionally.

Guarding your heart and mind means paying attention to what you allow in and how you care for what's already there. It may look like counseling, rest, rhythms of prayer, time in Scripture, healthy relationships, and wise boundaries with technology and media.

You can't lead others into clarity if you live in constant mental chaos. You can't make sound decisions if you're always overwhelmed. Protecting your mental strength is not selfish; it's stewardship. The people you lead need a grounded, clear, and healthy you.

Reflection Questions

1. What mental strengthening practices do I need to add or restore?

2. What drains my mental strength the fastest — and how can I limit it?

Author Quote — Coach David Angeron

"Mental strength isn't automatic — it's trained."

OCTOBER

FAITH, FAMILY & PERSONAL LIFE

OCTOBER 1 —
FAITH REQUIRES MOVEMENT

"Faith without works is dead." — James 2:17

Faith isn't belief alone — it's belief in motion. You can read, pray, plan, and prepare, but at some point faith has to put on shoes and move. Bold prayers must be backed by bold steps. You don't need a five-year plan to obey God today. You don't need every answer to take the next right step.

God rarely shows the whole path in advance; He reveals it step by step as you move. Many leaders stay stuck, asking God for more clarity, while God is waiting for more obedience. Faith says, "I don't see everything yet, but I trust the One who does."

Stagnation often disguises itself as overthinking. At some point, you must act on what you already know. Faith is not reckless — it is responsive. When God speaks, faith doesn't just nod in agreement; it walks in alignment.

Faith acts before certainty arrives.

Reflection Questions

1. What step have I been delaying even though I know God is calling me to take it?

2. What action today would demonstrate faith rather than fear?

Author Quote — Coach David Angeron

"Faith doesn't wait for clarity — it creates it."

October 2 — Purpose Requires Obedience When It's Difficult

"Whoever wants to be my disciple must deny themselves and take up their cross."
— Luke 9:23

Purpose is beautiful when we talk about it — but it's costly when we walk in it. The call of God doesn't just lead to open doors and opportunities; it also leads through sacrifice, stretching, and surrender. Sometimes obedience means saying no to what is easy so you can say yes to what is eternal.

God never promised the path would be painless — He promised it would be worth it. Your flesh will always reach for comfort. Your spirit must reach for calling. There will be moments when obedience feels like loss: loss of convenience, approval, or familiar routines. But what looks like loss is actually alignment.

Obedience opens doors that comfort never will. Destiny hinges on daily decisions to follow Jesus even when it costs you something. Purpose becomes powerful when it's no longer theory — it's personal, sacrificial, and lived.

Reflection Questions

1. Where have I chosen comfort over calling?

2. What difficult choice is actually obedience in disguise?

Author Quote — Coach David Angeron

"Purpose becomes powerful only after it becomes personal."

OCTOBER 3 — GOD GIVES VISION BEFORE PROVISION

"Write the vision and make it plain." — Habakkuk 2:2

When God gives you a vision, He rarely hands you a full budget and a finished blueprint. He gives direction first, then provision follows obedience, stewardship, and faith. Vision is God's way of saying, "This is where I'm taking you." Provision is His way of saying, "Now that you've started, I'll supply what you need."

If you wait until you have everything before you begin, you will never begin. Many leaders stall because they're staring at what they lack instead of using what they have. God often multiplies what's already in your hand — not what you're still waiting for.

Write the vision. Clarify it. Pray over it. Share it faithfully. Then start building with what you already possess: your time, relationships, skills, creativity, and small resources. Movement signals faith.

If God gave you the vision, God will fund the mission — but He often funds it along the journey, not before the first step.

Reflection Questions

1. Have I been waiting for resources before taking action?

2. What can I start building with what I already have?

Author Quote — Coach David Angeron

"Provision follows obedience — not hesitation."

October 4 — When God Opens a Door, Walk Through It Boldly

God doesn't open doors so you can stand in the hallway and analyze them. He opens doors for movement. Too often, leaders pray for opportunity and then freeze when it finally appears. Fear starts whispering: *What if I fail? What if I'm not ready? What if people don't approve?*

But if God opened the door, He already accounted for your weakness, your learning curve, and your need for grace. No person, critic, or circumstance can shut what He has sovereignly opened. The only one who can keep you from walking through is you.

Boldness is not arrogance — it's confidence in the One who unlocked the opportunity. Walk in knowing: you didn't open this door, and you don't have to sustain it. Your job is obedience. God's job is outcome.

Don't approach a God-given opportunity like it's a mistake.

Reflection Questions

1. What open door am I walking through timidly instead of boldly?
2. What fear is stopping me from stepping into a God-given opportunity?

Author Quote — Coach David Angeron

"Don't tiptoe through doors God called you to run through."

October 5 — Purpose Will Require You to Leave Your Comfort Zone

"Go from your country... to the land I will show you." — Genesis 12:1

Every major move of God in Scripture began with someone leaving the familiar. Abraham had to leave his homeland. Peter had to step out of the boat. The disciples had to leave their nets. Comfort is the enemy of progress because it convinces you that survival is enough.

But purpose doesn't grow in the soil of comfort. It grows in the soil of obedience, even when that obedience feels scary. Answering God's call may mean leaving certain surroundings, habits, circles, or patterns that once felt safe. It may mean embracing new environments where you feel inexperienced, stretched, and dependent on God in new ways.

Growth starts at the edge of discomfort. The part of you that wants to stay where it's easy must surrender to the part of you that wants to see everything God promised.

Reflection Questions

1. What comfort is holding me back from my calling?

2. What new environment, opportunity, or challenge do I need to embrace?

Author Quote — Coach David Angeron

"Purpose begins where comfort ends."

OCTOBER 6 —
DON'T DOUBT IN DELAY WHAT GOD PROMISED IN PRAYER

"Though it linger, wait for it; it will certainly come and will not delay."
— Habakkuk 2:3

Delay is one of the enemy's favorite tools to plant doubt. You pray in faith, but when the answer doesn't arrive quickly, your mind starts to question: *Did I hear God correctly? Did I mess this up? Has God forgotten me?* Yet Scripture is clear — some promises have an appointed time.

While you're waiting on the blessing, God is often working on the builder — you. Waiting seasons are not wasted seasons when you lean into them. They develop patience, character, wisdom, humility, and deeper dependence. Fruit takes time to grow, and so do leaders.

Don't interpret silence as abandonment or delay as denial. If God confirmed it in prayer, stand on it in patience. Let the waiting deepen your faith instead of draining it.

Reflection Questions

1. Where has delay made me doubt instead of develop?
2. How can I turn frustration into faith during waiting seasons?

Author Quote — Coach David Angeron

"Delay is not God ignoring you — it's God preparing you."

OCTOBER 7 — FAITH REQUIRES RISK

"We live by faith, not by sight." — 2 Corinthians 5:7

If your decisions require no risk, they require no faith. Faith doesn't mean recklessness — but it does mean you will step into places where outcomes aren't guaranteed and comfort isn't promised. You will make moves that don't make sense to everyone else but are clear in your spirit.

A safe life may protect you from failure, but it will also protect you from destiny. Playing it safe keeps you in what you can control; faith moves you into what only God can do. The question is not, "Is there risk?" The question is, "Is God leading?"

Faith steps forward when sight says, "Wait." It applies wisdom, counts the cost, and still chooses obedience when God says go. Every major breakthrough in your life will likely be connected to a moment when you decided to trust God more than you feared the risk.

Reflection Questions

1. What step am I afraid to take because it's risky?
2. What would I do if I trusted God more than I feared failure?

Author Quote — Coach David Angeron

"Faith doesn't eliminate risk — it overrides it."

October 8 — Don't Let Fear Become Your Decision-Maker

"For God has not given us a spirit of fear." — 2 Timothy 1:7

F ear is a loud advisor but a terrible leader. It constantly asks, *What if you fail? What if they reject you? What if it all falls apart?* If you're not careful, fear will become the unspoken counselor behind every decision you make.

Faith asks a different question: *What if God shows up in ways I never imagined? What if this step unlocks someone else's breakthrough? What if obedience leads to impact I can't see yet?*

You will feel fear — that's normal. The problem is not feeling fear; it's following fear. When fear becomes your decision-maker, you will shrink your calling to fit your comfort. When faith leads, fear can speak but it doesn't get to vote.

Your assignment is too important to hand the steering wheel to fear.

Reflection Questions

1. Have I made any recent decisions based on fear instead of faith?
2. What would I choose differently if fear wasn't in the equation?

Author Quote — Coach David Angeron

"Fear whispers limitations — faith declares possibilities."

October 9 — Your Calling Will Require Courage Before Evidence

"Blessed is she who believed that the Lord would fulfill His promises."
— Luke 1:45

God often asks you to move before there's any visible sign that things will work out. Mary believed the promise before she saw the miracle. Noah built the ark before it rained. Abraham walked toward a land he had never seen. Calling always requires courage before evidence.

If you're waiting for proof, you'll stay where you are. Kingdom leaders are called to believe before they see, obey before they feel ready, and act before there are guarantees. Evidence will come later — in testimonies, transformed lives, open doors, and unexpected provision.

Faith is not pretending everything looks good; it's trusting God when nothing looks finished. Heaven celebrates the leader who says, "God, if You said it, I will move like it's already done."

Reflection Questions

1. Where am I waiting for proof before moving?

2. What would courageous obedience look like right now?

Author Quote — Coach David Angeron

"Faith is acting like it's done even when nothing looks finished."

October 10 — Not Everyone Will Understand Your Calling — and That's Okay

"A prophet is not without honor except in his own town." — Matthew 13:57

Sometimes the people who know your history struggle the most to recognize your destiny. They remember your mistakes, your immaturity, your process — and have difficulty seeing your calling. That's not new; Jesus Himself was misunderstood and minimized in His hometown.

Your assignment from God does not require unanimous approval. If you wait for everyone to understand, agree, and cheer before you obey, you will never move. Some will question your decisions, misinterpret your motives, or resist the changes your obedience causes. That doesn't make your calling less real.

Honor people, but don't hand them the authority to veto what God has clearly spoken. Your job is not to convince everyone — it's to obey the One who called you.

Reflection Questions

1. Where have I delayed obedience while waiting for approval?

2. Whose opinion have I given too much influence over my calling?

Author Quote — Coach David Angeron

"Don't shrink your calling to fit someone else's comfort."

October 11 — Faith Moves Even When Conditions Aren't Ideal

"Whoever watches the wind will not plant." — Ecclesiastes 11:4

If you wait for perfect conditions, you'll never start. There will always be a reason to delay — not enough money, not enough time, not enough support, not enough clarity. Faith doesn't ignore reality, but it refuses to be paralyzed by it.

"Watching the wind" looks like obsessing over obstacles, overanalyzing risk, and waiting for a moment where every variable feels safe. That moment never comes. Farmers plant in uncertain weather. Leaders step out in uncertain seasons.

Faith asks, "What can I do today with what I have?" It doesn't deny the wind — it plants anyway. Progress in the kingdom doesn't come from perfect timing; it comes from courageous obedience in imperfect conditions.

Reflection Questions

1. What "perfect conditions" have I been waiting on?
2. What next step could I take today despite uncertainty?

Author Quote — Coach David Angeron

"If you wait for perfect, you'll miss your purpose."

October 12 —
Walk Through Doors God Opens — Even When You Feel Unqualified

"I can do all things through Christ who strengthens me." — Philippians 4:13

God rarely calls the most qualified on paper — He calls the most surrendered in spirit. If the opportunity feels bigger than you, that's often a sign it's from Him. He is not limited by your résumé, experience, or comfort level.

Feeling unqualified is human, but letting that feeling stop you is disobedience. What God initiates, God sustains. Grace meets you in the places your skill, confidence, and experience fall short. Growth happens when responsibility meets His strength.

You don't need confidence in yourself — you need confidence in the One who called you. Instead of saying, "I'm not enough," start saying, "He is enough, and He chose me for this."

Reflection Questions

1. What opportunity have I resisted because I felt unqualified?

2. What belief about myself needs to be replaced with belief in God?

Author Quote — Coach David Angeron

"If God called you to it, He already accounted for everything you lack."

October 13 — If God Gave the Vision, Don't Let People Set the Limit

People think within their limits; God speaks from His. When you share vision, some will respond from fear, past disappointments, or small thinking: *"That's too big... That's unrealistic... That's impossible."* But impossible to them is not impossible to God.

You can honor others' perspectives without surrendering to their limitations. Their doubt is a reflection of their ceiling, not God's capacity. If you aren't careful, you'll start shrinking God-sized vision to fit human-sized comfort.

If God gave the vision, hold it with conviction. Seek wise counsel, walk in humility, and make strategic plans — but don't let anyone talk you out of what God has already talked you into.

Reflection Questions

1. Whose doubt am I allowing to influence my direction?

2. What did God say that I need to believe again?

Author Quote — Coach David Angeron

"Don't accept limits God didn't authorize."

OCTOBER 14 —
PURSUE CALLING, NOT COMFORT

"Whoever wants to save their life will lose it, but whoever loses their life for me will find it." — Matthew 16:25

Comfort promises safety but quietly steals purpose. It convinces you that avoiding risk is the goal, that staying unchallenged is success. But Jesus teaches the opposite: the life you're trying to protect through comfort may be the very life you miss.

Calling will always stretch you beyond what feels manageable. It will require courage, sacrifice, faith, and surrender. It will ask you to step into rooms where you feel unprepared and moments where you must depend fully on God.

Comfort builds a life you can control. Calling builds a life only God can sustain. One leads to predictability; the other leads to impact. Choose carefully which one you chase.

Reflection Questions

1. Where have I chosen comfort instead of courage?

2. What discomfort might actually be preparation?

Author Quote — Coach David Angeron

"Comfort builds a life you can manage — calling builds a life only God can sustain."

October 15 — Don't Hesitate When God Says Go

"Obedience is better than sacrifice." — 1 Samuel 15:22

Delayed obedience often becomes disobedience. You can talk about God's instruction, analyze it, pray about it again, and ask five more people for confirmation — but at some point, God isn't asking for another discussion; He's asking for a decision.

Hesitation can be more damaging than an honest mistake. God can redirect a moving leader, but it's hard to steer someone who refuses to move. When God says "go," the safest place you can be is in motion — even if you don't feel fully ready.

Obedience unlocks opportunity, alignment, and favor that endless hesitation never will. Every time you respond quickly to God's voice, your sensitivity to His leading grows stronger.

Reflection Questions

1. What instruction from God have I delayed acting on?
2. What is one step of obedience I can take today?

Author Quote — Coach David Angeron

"Delayed obedience is expensive obedience."

October 16 — Faith Turns the Impossible Into the Inevitable

"Nothing will be impossible for you." — Matthew 17:20

Faith doesn't make life easy — it makes it unstoppable. Jesus never promised a life without obstacles; He promised that, with faith, those obstacles would not have the final word. When faith is active, what looks impossible by human standards becomes inevitable by kingdom standards.

Faith doesn't deny the size of the mountain — it recognizes the power of the God who moves it. It doesn't mean you ignore facts; it means you submit those facts to a greater truth. The doctor's report is real, the financial pressure is real, the opposition is real — but so is the authority of God.

Faith is not magic; it's partnership. You bring belief, obedience, and action. God brings strength, strategy, favor, and supernatural outcome. Over time, what once terrified you becomes part of your testimony. The very thing that tried to block you becomes the platform where God's power is revealed.

Faith doesn't ignore reality — it invites God to rewrite it.

Reflection Questions

1. What "impossible" situation do I need to bring to God again?

2. What would I attempt if I truly believed God was with me?

Author Quote — Coach David Angeron

"Faith doesn't ignore reality — it invites God to rewrite it."

OCTOBER 17 — STOP PLAYING SMALL

"Enlarge the place of your tent." — Isaiah 54:2

God did not create you to blend in with mediocrity. He created you to carry influence, impact, and kingdom assignments that require boldness. Playing small may feel safe, but it is a subtle form of disobedience when God has called you to more.

Playing small looks like shrinking your ideas so people won't feel uncomfortable, downplaying your calling so you don't get criticized, or ignoring your gifts so you don't have to risk failure. But you weren't given those gifts for hiding — you were given them for building.

Faith stretches you. It enlarges your thinking, your praying, your planning, and your expectations. When God says "enlarge," He is inviting you to prepare for more: more responsibility, more impact, more people to serve. That requires courage, not caution.

You honor God not by minimizing what He put in you, but by maximizing it for His glory. You are called to lead courageously, not cautiously.

Reflection Questions

1. Where have I played small to avoid criticism or discomfort?

2. What bold step would match the size of the calling on my life?

Author Quote — Coach David Angeron

"You weren't called to fit in — you were called to stand out."

October 18 — When God Calls, Don't Count Yourself Out

When God sent Samuel to anoint the next king, everyone assumed the choice would be the strongest, oldest, or most impressive brother. God chose David — the overlooked shepherd. Heaven's selection criteria look nothing like human metrics.

We often do to ourselves what David's family did to him: we count ourselves out before we ever step up. We replay our failures, weaknesses, lack of credentials, or late start and assume we're disqualified. But God isn't scanning your résumé — He's searching your heart.

He looks for willingness, humility, obedience, and faith. If God has called you, He has already taken your flaws, fears, and history into account. You see limitation; He sees preparation. You see insecurity; He sees dependency.

Stop disqualifying what God has already decided. The question isn't, "Am I enough?" The question is, "Will I say yes?"

Reflection Questions

1. What insecurity has been holding me back from stepping into my calling?

2. What evidence has God shown that I am chosen and capable?

Author Quote — Coach David Angeron

"God didn't make a mistake when He picked you."

October 19 —

A Faithless Environment Will Suffocate a Faith-Filled Vision

Vision is fragile in its early stages. When God first places something in your heart, it often feels bigger than your capacity and far beyond your current reality. In that vulnerable phase, the environment you share it in matters.

Some people don't attack you because they're evil; they attack because they're limited. They respond through their own fear, insecurity, or lack of belief. They'll say, "That's too big... too risky... too unrealistic." If you allow those voices too much access, their doubt will start to smother your faith.

Discernment means knowing who can handle the weight of what God showed you. Share your vision with people who pray, build, strategize, and encourage — not with those who gossip, mock, or minimize. Your assignment is sacred. Protect it like it is.

Discernment protects destiny.

Reflection Questions

1. Who strengthens my faith — and who weakens it?

2. Who can I trust with the vision God gave me?

Author Quote — Coach David Angeron

"Share your vision with builders — not doubters."

307

October 20 — God Will Confirm What He Called You To

"My sheep listen to my voice." — John 10:27

G od is not vague about what truly matters. When He calls you, He doesn't leave you wandering in constant confusion. He confirms — through Scripture that jumps off the page, peace that doesn't match the circumstance, mentors who echo what God already whispered, doors that open unexpectedly, or burdens that won't leave your heart.

Calling may stretch you, but it won't be chaos. You might feel unqualified or nervous, but there will be a deep sense of "this is right" in your spirit. That inner witness is not emotion — it's the Holy Spirit.

Sometimes we say, "I'm waiting for confirmation," when God has already confirmed multiple times — we just want a more comfortable assignment. Look back: what patterns, nudges, and moments has God used to repeatedly point you in the same direction?

Confirmation always follows obedience — and often increases after you start moving.

Reflection Questions

1. Has God already confirmed my calling in ways I've overlooked?

2. What sign of confirmation have I been waiting on unnecessarily?

Author Quote — Coach David Angeron

"When God speaks, He also confirms."

October 21 —
Purpose Requires Priorities

"Teach us to number our days." — Psalm 90:12

Y ou have the capacity to do many things — but you don't have the time to do everything. Purpose isn't fulfilled by accident; it's fulfilled by alignment. Every yes you give is a withdrawal from your time, energy, and focus. If you don't choose your priorities, distractions will choose them for you.

Purpose requires you to decide what matters most — and then live like it. That may mean saying no to good opportunities that don't fit your assignment. It may mean restructuring your calendar, limiting certain relationships, or changing how you use your free time.

Numbering your days is about recognizing their value. You don't have an endless supply, so you can't afford to waste them on everything that screams for attention but doesn't serve your calling.

Purpose is not achieved by raw effort; it's achieved when your efforts match your God-given priorities.

Reflection Questions

1. What distractions have been pulling attention away from my calling?

2. What priority shift could create more purpose and progress?

Author Quote — Coach David Angeron

"Purpose isn't achieved by effort — it's achieved by alignment."

October 22 — Faith Turns Pressure Into Progress

"Trials produce perseverance." — Romans 5:3

Pressure is part of every leader's story — but how you interpret it determines whether it breaks you or builds you. Without faith, pressure feels like punishment. With faith, pressure looks like preparation.

God uses pressure to expose what needs strengthening, trimming, or realigning. Under pressure, you discover where your character is solid and where it's shaky, where your systems are strong and where they're fragile. Pressure forces refinement — in priorities, relationships, habits, and mindsets.

The very weight you're resenting might be developing the exact capacity you'll need for the next level. Instead of asking, "Why is this happening to me?" start asking, "What is God building in me through this?"

Faith doesn't always remove pressure, but it repurposes it. What once felt like a burden becomes a training ground for greater influence.

Reflection Questions

1. How has pressure shaped my character recently?

2. What would happen if I embraced pressure instead of resenting it?

Author Quote — Coach David Angeron

"Pressure isn't crushing you — it's constructing you."

October 23 — Faith Doesn't Eliminate Fear — It Overrules It

The existence of fear in your life doesn't mean you lack faith — it means you're human. The question isn't, "Do I feel fear?" The real question is, "Who gets the final say — fear or faith?"

Faith doesn't always silence fear instantly, but it chooses obedience despite fear. David didn't fight Goliath because he felt zero fear; he fought because he had greater confidence in God than in the giant. Courage is not a feeling — it is a decision backed by trust.

You may still feel nervous, uncertain, or unqualified when you step out, but faith says, "I hear you, fear — but you're not in charge." Over time, as you repeatedly choose faith-led actions, fear's grip weakens and your confidence in God strengthens.

Fear may speak — but faith makes the decision.

Reflection Questions

1. Where have I mistaken fear as a sign to stop instead of a sign to trust?

2. What obedience step can I take even if fear is still present?

Author Quote — Coach David Angeron

"Courage isn't the lack of fear — it's leadership over fear."

OCTOBER 24 — DO THE NATURAL — GOD WILL DO THE SUPERNATURAL

"Stretch out your hand." — Exodus 14:16

Throughout Scripture, God attaches miracles to simple acts of obedience. Moses stretched out his hand, and God parted the sea. The widow poured oil, and God multiplied it. The servants filled jars with water, and Jesus turned it into wine. God asks for what you can do — then He does what only He can do.

Sometimes we're waiting on a miracle while God is waiting on a movement. We pray for breakthrough but resist the practical step: the call, the application, the conversation, the planning, the repentance, the act of faith that seems too small to matter.

Faith is not passive. It doesn't sit back and say, "If God wants it done, He'll do it." Faith says, "Because God wants it done, I'll do my part — and trust Him with the outcome."

You do what you can; God does what you can't.

Reflection Questions

1. What action step has God asked me to take before the miracle?

2. Where do I need to participate instead of waiting passively?

Author Quote — Coach David Angeron

"Miracles meet obedience at the intersection of faith and action."

October 25 — Don't Let Temporary Resistance Cause Permanent Retreat

"Do not grow weary in doing good." — Galatians 6:9

R esistance is often a sign that you're moving in the right direction, not the wrong one. The enemy doesn't waste energy attacking what isn't advancing. When you step into calling, fight for purity, build something kingdom-focused, or lead with conviction, opposition will show up.

If you interpret every obstacle as a "no" from God, you'll retreat from the very places you were assigned to occupy. Resistance may come through circumstances, criticism, spiritual warfare, or simple fatigue — but it doesn't mean "stop." It often means "press."

Perseverance is the separator between those who dream and those who see destiny realized. The ground you're standing on today may be the very place you once prayed to reach. Don't abandon it because it's harder than you expected.

Reflection Questions

1. Has resistance made me question what God already confirmed?

2. What would perseverance look like today?

Author Quote — Coach David Angeron

"Resistance isn't rejection — it's proof that progress is happening."

OCTOBER 26 —
THE REWARD IS WORTH THE RISK

"For at the proper time we will reap a harvest if we do not give up."
— Galatians 6:9

Every calling comes with a cost. You sacrifice time, comfort, energy, reputation, and sometimes relationships. You endure seasons of obscurity, misunderstanding, and spiritual warfare. There will be days you ask, "Is it worth it?"

God's answer is always yes. The harvest of obedience — lives changed, families impacted, souls reached, legacies rewritten, and faith strengthened — is worth every risk and every tear. The reward isn't just earthly results; it's knowing you did what heaven asked you to do.

The enemy wants you to quit right before the harvest hits full maturity. But Scripture promises "at the proper time." That means God has already circled harvest days on heaven's calendar. Your job is to not walk off the field before they arrive.

Reflection Questions

1. What reward am I believing God for in this season?

2. What daily discipline will keep me moving toward the harvest?

Author Quote — Coach David Angeron

"When it's all said and done, obedience pays more than fear ever could."

October 27 — You Can't Pray for Growth and Stay the Same

"Faith by itself, if it is not accompanied by action, is dead." — James 2:17

You can't ask God for next-level influence while clinging to first-level habits. Growth is not just something God does around you — it's something He does in you. That means things must change: your thinking, your routines, your disciplines, your boundaries, your responses.

Praying for growth without being willing to be stretched is like asking for harvest without planting seeds. God will answer your prayer for growth by inviting you into processes that challenge your comfort, expose your weaknesses, and refine your character.

New levels don't come with old patterns. You can't carry yesterday's excuses into tomorrow's assignment. The leader you're becoming requires decisions the old you would avoid. Your prayer must sound like: "Lord, grow my impact — and grow me with it."

Reflection Questions

1. What habit or mindset must I release to grow?

2. What does the next-level version of me consistently do?

Author Quote — Coach David Angeron

"You can't step into the new while holding on to the familiar."

OCTOBER 28 —
YOUR CALLING IS NOT FRAGILE

"The gifts and calling of God are irrevocable." — Romans 11:29

God's calling on your life is not glass — it doesn't shatter every time you stumble. You can make mistakes, take detours, walk through dark seasons, and still find God's purpose waiting on the other side. His calling is anchored in His faithfulness, not your perfection.

You may have delayed obedience. You may have allowed fear, sin, or distraction to derail you for a season. But the fact that you're still breathing is proof that God is not finished. The enemy loves to say, "It's too late. You blew it." Scripture says, "The calling is irrevocable."

Your setbacks didn't surprise God. He knew every failure you would experience and still chose you. Calling can be buried under shame, disappointment, or self-doubt — but it is never canceled. It's time to believe again.

Reflection Questions

1. Where have I believed my mistakes disqualified my calling?

2. What would I pursue if I truly believed the calling is still active?

Author Quote — Coach David Angeron

"Your calling is stronger than your setbacks."

OCTOBER 29 — DON'T ASK FOR MIRACLES IF YOU WON'T MAKE MOVES

Miracles and movement go together. You can't pray for God to open doors while refusing to walk toward them. You can't ask for increase without being willing to sow, build, learn, risk, and obey.

Many believers are frustrated not because God is absent, but because their faith is inactive. Faith without works is not faith at all — it's agreement without engagement. Heaven responds powerfully when you move in alignment with what you've prayed.

If you're believing for financial breakthrough, are you stewarding well? If you're believing for new opportunities, are you preparing your skills? If you're believing for restored relationships, are you willing to forgive, initiate, or have hard conversations?

Faith talks to God — but it also walks with God. Miracles often meet you halfway, in motion.

Reflection Questions

1. What miracle am I praying for that also requires my action?

2. What step of faith can I take today — even if small?

Author Quote — Coach David Angeron

"Miracles meet momentum."

October 30 — Faith Doesn't Guarantee Easy — It Guarantees Victory

"In this world you will have trouble. But take heart! I have overcome the world."
— John 16:33

Faith is not a shield from all hardship — it's a guarantee that hardship doesn't win. Jesus didn't say, "You might have trouble." He said, "You will." But He followed it with, "Take heart. I have overcome."

Faith doesn't mean you won't feel pressure, grief, loss, or conflict. It means none of those things have the final say. Victory is not the absence of battles; it's the assurance that, through Christ, every battle must bow to His authority.

Sometimes we interpret difficulty as failure, assuming, "If this were really God, it wouldn't be this hard." In reality, many of the most God-ordained assignments in Scripture were the most opposed. Your struggle doesn't mean you're off track — it may mean you're right where you're supposed to be.

Reflection Questions

1. Have I misinterpreted difficulty as failure?
2. What victory do I need to declare even before I see it?

Author Quote — Coach David Angeron

"Faith doesn't deny battles — it declares victory before the battle is over."

OCTOBER 31 — DON'T SLOW DOWN WHEN BREAKTHROUGH IS NEAR

"Let us run with perseverance the race marked out for us." — Hebrews 12:1

The last stretch of any race is always the hardest — not because you're weak, but because you're close. In the kingdom, resistance often intensifies right before breakthrough. Doors feel heavier, opposition feels louder, and weariness feels deeper.

The enemy hopes you'll interpret this pressure as a sign to stop. But often, it's the opposite — it's evidence that the finish line of this season is near. Many leaders slow down, compromise, or quit right when perseverance would have carried them into the very promise they've been praying for.

Don't judge your progress only by how you feel. Judge it by your faithfulness. If God has not told you to stop, keep running. Adjust your pace, replenish your strength, ask for help — but don't walk away.

You're closer than you think.

Reflection Questions

1. Where have I felt increased resistance that might actually signal breakthrough?

2. What discipline, commitment, or obedience must continue?

Author Quote — Coach David Angeron

"The greatest pressure often comes right before the promise."

NOVEMBER

LEGACY, IMPACT & CALLING

November 1 —
You Are Called to Leave Earth
Better Than You Found It

"A good person leaves an inheritance to their children's children."
— Proverbs 13:22

L egacy is not just about what people inherit in your name — it's about who they become because you lived. God's idea of inheritance goes far beyond money, property, and possessions. It includes faith, wisdom, courage, work ethic, integrity, and spiritual covering.

You are not here just to make a living; you are here to make a difference. Every decision, conversation, and opportunity is a chance to plant seeds that will outlive you. When your life is over, people won't remember every accomplishment, but they will remember how you loved, how you served, how you forgave, and how you pointed them to Jesus.

Legacy is not something that suddenly appears at the end of life — it's something you are building right now with your daily choices. You are writing your future remembrance in real time.

Your life is not just for you — it's for those coming after you.

Reflection Questions

1. What values do I want to be remembered for most?

2. Am I living daily in a way that builds spiritual legacy?

Author Quote — Coach David Angeron

"Legacy is not something you leave behind —
it's something you live until your last breath."

November 2 —
Multiply What God Gave You

"Well done... you have been faithful with a few things." — Matthew 25:21

In the parable of the talents, the Master didn't applaud the servant who buried what he was given. He celebrated the ones who multiplied it. That story isn't just about money — it's about everything God has put in your hands: your skills, calling, network, experiences, platform, and influence.

He didn't give you those things to be protected by fear or hidden behind insecurity. He expects growth. Playing small, staying safe, and avoiding risk may feel responsible, but heaven calls that "burying" what you were meant to build.

Multiplication looks like mentoring others, starting what God told you to start, writing the book, launching the vision, refining your craft, and using your influence to advance the kingdom. Productivity in the kingdom is not about busyness — it's about fruitfulness.

God doesn't reward potential — He rewards productivity.

Reflection Questions

1. What gift or opportunity have I buried out of fear?
2. How can I multiply what God has trusted me with?

Author Quote — Coach David Angeron

"The Master isn't looking for preservation — He's looking for multiplication."

November 3 — Legacy Requires Generational Vision

"One generation will commend Your works to another." — Psalm 145:4

Most people plan for the weekend; a few plan for the year; very few plan for generations. Legacy leaders think beyond their lifetime. They ask: "What will continue because I was obedient?"

Generational vision doesn't mean you see every detail; it means you build with "beyond me" in mind. You lead, structure, and invest so that what God started with you doesn't die with you. That may include documenting systems, training successors, empowering younger leaders, or building teams that don't depend on your personality to survive.

If everything you're building collapses when you step away, it wasn't legacy — it was dependency. Kingdom leadership is succession-minded. You're not just creating impact; you're creating carriers who will pass the mission down the line.

The greatest leaders build succession, not dependency.

Reflection Questions

1. Am I building something that depends on me or something that outlives me?

2. Who must I invest in to carry the mission forward?

Author Quote — Coach David Angeron

"Legacy begins when leadership becomes bigger than one lifetime."

November 4 — Legacy Is Built by Consistency, Not Occasions

You won't be remembered for a few big moments nearly as much as you'll be remembered for the person you were every day. Grand gestures are impressive — but daily consistency is what changes lives.

Legacy is built in the small, repeated things: praying over your family, showing up with integrity, keeping your word, leading with character, honoring God in private, and loving people when it's inconvenient. It is formed when your actions align with your values over and over again.

Occasional greatness can inspire people for a moment; consistent faithfulness shapes them for a lifetime. Repetition creates remembrance. The habits you hold onto today will become the stories people tell about you tomorrow.

Don't underestimate the quiet, steady choices you're making — they are building a legacy brick by brick.

Reflection Questions

1. What consistent habit is shaping the legacy I'm building?

2. What inconsistency could damage the legacy I desire?

Author Quote — Coach David Angeron

"Legacy isn't a moment — it's a lifestyle."

November 5 — Legacy Is Who You Become, Not What You Accumulate

"Surely goodness and love will follow me all the days of my life." — Psalm 23:6

When your life is over, people won't line up to talk about your car, your house, or your bank account. They will talk about your character. They will remember how you made them feel, how you showed up, how you treated people who could do nothing for you.

The real measure of wealth is not in what you own but in what follows you: goodness, love, generosity, wisdom, and faith. That's what Psalm 23 describes — a life so aligned with God that His goodness and mercy "follow" you. That's legacy.

You have permission to pursue success — but never at the expense of who you're becoming. Legacy is the person God shapes you into as you walk with Him. Your titles will fade. Your true inheritance will be the impact of a Christ-shaped life.

A legacy is a life that echoes.

Reflection Questions

1. What part of my life leaves the loudest echo today?
2. What trait do I want others to receive from my example?

Author Quote — Coach David Angeron

"Your greatest inheritance is not in your bank — it's in your influence."

November 6 — Your Life Is a Message Someone Else Will Follow

"Follow my example, as I follow the example of Christ." — 1 Corinthians 11:1

You don't need a microphone to preach — your life already is. Someone is watching you while they learn how to respond to pressure, handle disappointment, manage success, treat people, handle conflict, and walk with God.

Legacy is not just what you say; it's what you display. Every choice is a sentence in the story people are reading about you. Your reactions are lessons, your priorities are teaching points, and your faithfulness in hard seasons is a blueprint for someone else's survival.

This doesn't mean living under pressure to be perfect — it means living with awareness and intentionality. You are not responsible to impress people; you are responsible to influence them toward Christ.

You are writing a manual for someone's future without even speaking. Make sure the message matches the mission.

Reflection Questions

1. What message is my daily life preaching to those watching me?

2. What adjustment would strengthen the example I'm setting?

Author Quote — Coach David Angeron

"Your life is a textbook someone else is studying."

November 7 —
Legacy Begins at Home

"But as for me and my household, we will serve the Lord." — Joshua 24:15

It is possible to be admired publicly and absent privately. You can build a ministry, business, or platform and neglect the people living under your own roof. That is not success — that is imbalance.

Legacy begins where your last name lives. Before you lead teams, you lead your home. Before you inspire crowds, you invest in your spouse, children, and family. Your greatest testimony is not what the world says about you — it's what your family can honestly say about your character.

The people closest to you should not only know your vision, but also feel your love, presence, and spiritual covering. Don't give the world your best and your family your leftovers. Impact that doesn't touch home is incomplete.

The greatest leadership happens off the stage and inside the home.

Reflection Questions

1. Does my family get the best of me or the leftovers of me?

2. What can I do this week to strengthen love and presence at home?

Author Quote — Coach David Angeron

"Legacy is powerful when your family can testify of your character."

November 8 — Legacy Requires Intentional Investment

"Teach them to your children and to their children after them."
— Deuteronomy 4:9

Values don't automatically transfer — they must be intentionally taught, modeled, and reinforced. If you don't disciple your children, mentees, and team, culture, social media, and confusion will gladly do it for you.

Intentional investment looks like conversations, prayers, corrections, encouragements, and time. It looks like explaining not just "what" you do, but "why" you do it. It looks like allowing people to see both your victories and vulnerability so they can learn from your process, not just your outcomes.

Legacy doesn't happen by default; it happens by design. You must decide what matters most — faith, integrity, excellence, courage, generosity — and then actively deposit those values into others.

Legacy is built through intentional transfer.

Reflection Questions

1. Who am I intentionally mentoring, teaching, or guiding?

2. What value do I want to transfer before anything else?

Author Quote — Coach David Angeron

"Legacy isn't what you leave to people — it's what you leave in people."

November 9 — What You Build With God Will Outlast You

You can spend your life building something impressive — and still miss building something eternal. Human ambition can create big platforms, but only God partnership creates lasting impact. When God is the architect, what you build carries His fingerprint and His staying power.

Building with God means you invite Him into the vision, the planning, the decisions, the pace, and the motives. It means praying over your work, aligning it with His Word, and being willing to shift when He redirects.

When He builds through you, the work doesn't collapse when you're gone. It continues in the people, systems, and seeds you planted in obedience. You don't need to be remembered if Jesus is revealed.

You don't have to build fast — you have to build faithfully. Eternal work is never wasted work.

Reflection Questions

1. Am I building my name or God's kingdom?
2. Is the foundation of my work rooted in prayer and obedience?

Author Quote — Coach David Angeron

"When God builds it through you, it continues beyond you."

November 10 — Legacy Requires Finishing Well, Not Just Starting Strong

"I have fought the good fight, I have finished the race." — 2 Timothy 4:7

Starting is exciting — finishing is rare. Many people begin with zeal, passion, and big dreams, but along the way, distractions, disappointments, and fatigue tempt them to quit. Legacy belongs to those who keep going.

Finishing well doesn't mean you never stumbled — it means you got back up. It doesn't mean the race was smooth — it means you ran the race God assigned to you, with perseverance and faith. Paul didn't brag about how fast he ran; he celebrated that he finished the race and kept the faith.

Finishing well might look like staying faithful in your marriage, persevering through a long assignment, transitioning leadership with integrity, or closing a chapter without bitterness.

Don't just run fast — run faithful.

Reflection Questions

1. Where has passion faded and discipline must now take over?

2. What would finishing well look like in this chapter of my life?

Author Quote — Coach David Angeron

"Anyone can start — legacy belongs to those who finish."

November 11 — Your Pain Can Become Someone Else's Roadmap

"He comforts us... so that we can comfort those in any trouble."
— 2 Corinthians 1:4

The battles you've walked through were never just about you. God comforted, carried, and restored you so you could do the same for others. Your pain, processed in His presence, becomes wisdom. Your scars become signposts.

Someone is currently fighting a battle you've already survived: a setback, betrayal, financial strain, burnout, grief, or disappointment. Legacy means you don't hide your testimony — you steward it. You allow God to use your story as a map for someone still trying to find their way out.

This doesn't mean glorifying your past; it means glorifying God's faithfulness in it. When you courageously share how He met you in your lowest places, others find courage to believe He can meet them in theirs.

Your breakthrough becomes someone's blueprint.

Reflection Questions

1. What past battle has equipped me to help others today?

2. Who could benefit from my testimony if I shared it?

Author Quote — Coach David Angeron

"Your wounds become wisdom when you're willing to share the story."

November 12 — Legacy Requires Sacrifice Today for Strength Tomorrow

"No discipline seems pleasant at the time, but painful. Later on, however, it produces a harvest of righteousness." — Hebrews 12:11

Legacy is not built in comfort — it's built in sacrifice. Every time you say no to flesh and yes to God, you plant seeds for future strength. Discipline may feel painful in the moment, but it produces a harvest that your children, team, and community will one day enjoy.

Sacrifice can look like saving instead of overspending, turning off distractions to invest in family, guarding your purity, showing up early, staying consistent in the Word, or walking away from opportunities that don't align with your values.

The enemy wants you obsessed with "now." Legacy leaders are focused on "later." They're willing to endure short-term discomfort for long-term blessing — not just for themselves, but for the generations to come.

Sacrifice may cost you now, but it pays generationally.

Reflection Questions

1. What short-term sacrifice will produce long-term legacy?
2. In which area of life do I need stronger self-discipline?

Author Quote — Coach David Angeron

"Sacrifice feels expensive now — generational blessing proves it was cheap."

November 13 — Leadership Without Legacy Is Just Labor

You can work hard your entire life and still miss what matters most. Leadership without eternal impact is just labor — activity without lasting significance. Jesus reminds us to store up treasures in heaven, not just on earth. That means investing in souls, discipleship, generosity, and kingdom work.

When your leadership is only about hitting numbers, building brands, or chasing status, you may succeed temporarily but remain empty eternally. Legacy shifts your focus from, "How much can I achieve?" to, "How much can I impact?"

Look at where your time, energy, and influence are going. Are they building something God cares about? Are they touching people, not just projects? Legacy isn't anti-success — it just insists that success serves a higher purpose.

Legacy turns labor into purpose.

Reflection Questions

1. Does my work lead to eternal impact or just temporary results?

2. Where can I intentionally serve beyond success?

Author Quote — Coach David Angeron

"Success is being remembered — legacy is being continued."

November 14 — Multiply Leaders, Not Dependents

True leadership doesn't thrive on people needing you — it thrives on people being equipped by you. In the kingdom, success is not measured by how many people depend on you, but by how many people are empowered to lead because of you.

If everything stops when you're absent, you haven't built a team — you've built dependency. Legacy-minded leaders train others to think, lead, decide, and carry the mission themselves. They share information, opportunities, and authority. They are not threatened by strong leaders; they produce them.

Multiplying leaders means giving people chances, coaching them through mistakes, and believing in them beyond their current level. It means shifting from "Do this for me" to "Let me teach you how to do this."

You are called to build people who build people.

Reflection Questions

1. Have I been developing independent leaders or dependent helpers?

2. Who can I elevate, empower, and equip more intentionally?

Author Quote — Coach David Angeron

"Leadership reproduces workers — legacy reproduces leaders."

November 15 — Legacy Is Measured by the People You Raised, Not the Things You Built

"Make disciples of all nations." — Matthew 28:19

Jesus didn't leave behind buildings, brands, or organizations — He left behind disciples. People carried His mission forward. That's the blueprint for legacy.

You can build impressive structures and systems, but if you don't build people, the work has no one to carry it into the future. Heaven's scoreboard isn't counting your projects; it's counting the lives you've discipled, mentored, coached, and developed.

Legacy asks, "Who am I raising up?" not just, "What am I building?" It redirects your energy from only tasks and timelines to hearts and minds. It reminds you that the most important thing you might do for God may not be something you do — it may be someone you train.

Legacy is not in monuments — it's in people.

Reflection Questions

1. Who am I intentionally discipling, mentoring, or developing?

2. What person — not project — needs my energy this week?

Author Quote — Coach David Angeron

"Legacy isn't counted in accomplishments — it's counted in people."

November 16 — A Legacy Leader Builds Bridges, Not Thrones

Some leaders are obsessed with building platforms that elevate their name. Legacy leaders are obsessed with building bridges that elevate others. A throne mindset asks, "How can people serve me?" A bridge mindset asks, "How can I make it easier for others to walk in their God-given calling?"

Jesus, the greatest leader who ever lived, didn't come to be served but to serve. He washed feet, empowered disciples, released people into ministry, and made room at the table for those others ignored. That's the blueprint of legacy leadership.

When your influence creates opportunities, pathways, exposure, and development for others, you're no longer just successful—you're significant. The question shifts from, "How high can I go?" to, "How many can I take with me?"

The mark of a great leader is not how high they climb — but how many they lift.

Reflection Questions

1. Am I building opportunities for others or only for myself?
2. Who can I empower or elevate today?

Author Quote — Coach David Angeron

"Legacy builds ladders for others to climb."

November 17 — Don't Rush Success — Build Sustainability

"By wisdom a house is built, and through understanding it is established."
— Proverbs 24:3

The world celebrates speed: fast growth, instant results, overnight success. But God celebrates wisdom, depth, and foundation. Anyone can rise quickly with enough hype and hustle—but what rises fast often falls even faster. Sustainable success is different. It's built brick by brick, with wisdom guiding every decision.

Legacy leaders resist the temptation to skip steps. They don't cut corners in character, team development, systems, or spiritual roots. They understand that what God builds slowly, He intends to stand firmly. Wisdom asks: "Will this still be standing in ten years?" not just "Will this impress people today?"

Rushing leads to cracks—spiritually, emotionally, financially, and organizationally. Wisdom takes the time to learn, adjust, prepare, and establish. Don't just aim to arrive; aim to remain.

Greatness built slowly lasts the longest.

Reflection Questions

1. Where have I been rushing progress rather than building strategically?

2. What long-term habit will produce long-term strength?

Author Quote — Coach David Angeron

"Success that happens slowly becomes success that lasts."

November 18 — Legacy Isn't Born in Comfort — It's Born in Consistency

"Whatever you do, work at it with all your heart." — Colossians 3:23

Comfort never built a legacy. It feels good, but it does not stretch you, train you, or transform you. Legacy grows in the grind—showing up when you're tired, staying faithful when the results are small, and giving your best when no one is clapping.

Consistency is where calling and character shake hands. God isn't just watching your big moments; He's watching your regular ones. The steady effort, the quiet obedience, the daily excellence—those are the building blocks of a life that echoes.

Motivation is helpful, but it's inconsistent. Some days you'll feel it, some days you won't. Consistency doesn't ask, "Do I feel like it?" It says, "I'm committed to it." When you work with all your heart as unto the Lord, even ordinary days become legacy days.

Consistency is your legacy's greatest ally.

Reflection Questions

1. Where do I need more consistency to honor the calling on my life?

2. What small discipline will have the biggest future impact?

Author Quote — Coach David Angeron

"Motivation fades — consistency finishes."

November 19 — Legacy Doesn't Happen Overnight — It Happens Over Time

"Do not despise these small beginnings." — Zechariah 4:10

We live in a world addicted to instant results. But God's way of building is often slow, steady, and intentional. Small beginnings are not insignificant beginnings—they are sacred. Those early chapters, where very few people notice, are where your discipline, humility, and endurance get forged.

Legacy isn't created by one viral moment, one big promotion, or one major opportunity. It's created by thousands of small choices: showing up on time, doing the right thing, serving faithfully, leading with integrity, and honoring God day after day.

Don't despise the season where things seem small, hidden, or unimpressive. This is where God is strengthening your foundation so you can handle what's coming. Today's unnoticed obedience is tomorrow's undeniable impact.

Don't underestimate the slow chapters — they're shaping the strong chapters.

Reflection Questions

1. Have I dismissed small progress because it wasn't dramatic?

2. What small step today contributes to long-term legacy?

Author Quote — Coach David Angeron

"Legacy is built by the seconds, not the spotlight."

November 20 — Legacy Requires Planting Seeds You May Never See Grow

"One plants, another waters, but God gives the increase." — 1 Corinthians 3:6

Legacy-minded leaders understand a powerful truth: you are part of a much bigger story. Some of what God asks you to do will not fully bloom in your lifetime. You may plant seeds in your children, students, athletes, staff, or community that generations after you will harvest.

That means you can't be addicted to immediate results. You mentor, teach, give, serve, build, and sow—even when you don't see the full fruit yet. Eternity keeps the record, and God brings the increase in His timing.

Legacy leadership is not about ownership; it's about obedience. You're willing to do the hidden work, knowing that someone else may carry the baton across the visible finish line. And you're okay with that, because the win belongs to the kingdom, not your ego.

Legacy leaders care more about the kingdom than credit.

Reflection Questions

1. What am I building that may benefit people I'll never meet?

2. Am I willing to sow where someone else will reap?

Author Quote — Coach David Angeron

"Legacy isn't measured by what you see — but by what you set in motion."

November 21 — The Enemy Fights the Hardest When Generations Will Be Impacted

The intensity of your spiritual warfare often reveals the importance of your assignment. When your obedience affects not just you—but your children, your team, your community, and future generations—the enemy takes notice. He's not just trying to discourage a person; he's trying to disrupt a legacy.

That's why attacks increase when you start breaking generational cycles, building kingdom work, or laying foundations that will outlive you. Increased pressure doesn't mean you're losing—it means your impact is dangerous to darkness.

In those seasons, you can't afford to retreat. You lean deeper into prayer, Scripture, wise counsel, and spiritual authority. You stand firm knowing that your perseverance isn't just for you—it's for those coming after you.

Don't back down — double down.

Reflection Questions

1. Where have I felt increased battles as my impact grows?

2. How can I respond with persistence instead of discouragement?

Author Quote — Coach David Angeron

"Your warfare reveals your worth."

November 22 — Legacy Is Not Perfection — It's Perseverance

"Though the righteous fall seven times, they rise again." — Proverbs 24:16

Legacy leaders are not the ones who never fall—they're the ones who refuse to stay down. Perfection has never built a legacy; perseverance has. God isn't looking for flawless leaders; He's looking for faithful ones.

You will make mistakes. You will misjudge situations. You will experience failures, disappointments, and moments you wish you could redo. But your legacy won't be defined by those falls—it will be defined by your response. Do you quit? Or do you rise, repent, learn, and keep moving forward?

Your resilience becomes a testimony. The next generation needs to see not just your victories, but your recoveries. They need to know that falling is not the end of the story when God is the Author.

Perseverance builds generational faith.

Reflection Questions

1. Where have I been too hard on myself while God is still calling me forward?

2. What does "getting back up" look like today?

Author Quote — Coach David Angeron

"Your legacy is not in your falls — it's in your comebacks."

November 23 — Don't Let Success Distract You From Significance

Success and significance are not the same. Success is often measured by numbers—revenue, results, recognition, reach. Significance is measured by impact—lives changed, faith strengthened, families restored, people discipled.

The danger is that success can become a distraction. You can chase awards, titles, and applause so aggressively that you drift from the original assignment God gave you. What the world applauds isn't always what heaven affirms.

Legacy leaders continually realign their hearts: "Am I just building something impressive, or something important? Something that looks good now, or something that matters forever?"

Significance often looks quieter than success—but it echoes longer. It may not always trend, but it will always bear fruit.

Choose significance over applause.

Reflection Questions

1. Am I chasing recognition or purpose?
2. What eternal impact am I pursuing right now?

Author Quote — Coach David Angeron

"Success fades — significance echoes."

November 24 — A True Legacy Points People to Jesus, Not to You

"He must become greater; I must become less." — John 3:30

God doesn't elevate you so people can be impressed with you—He elevates you so people can encounter Him. Influence is a stewardship, not a spotlight. Your leadership, platform, and achievements are meant to function like a mirror: reflecting the glory back to Jesus.

Legacy leaders are careful with credit. They deflect worship, honor God publicly, and make it clear that anything good in them is the result of His grace. They use their stories, success, and platforms as stages for the gospel—not for ego.

At the end of your life, the greatest compliment won't be "You were amazing," but "Because of you, I saw Jesus more clearly."

The goal is not to be remembered — the goal is to make Jesus known.

Reflection Questions

1. Do people see Jesus more clearly because of the way I lead?

2. How can I shift attention from me to Him with greater intentionality?

Author Quote — Coach David Angeron

*"The greatest legacy is when lives are changed because
they encountered Jesus through you."*

November 25 — Finish the Year With the Same Fire You Started With

"Whatever your hand finds to do, do it with all your might." — Ecclesiastes 9:10

It's easy to start a year full of vision, goals, and passion. It's harder to finish with that same intensity—especially after setbacks, detours, and disappointments. But legacy leaders don't coast into the finish line—they lean into it.

The final stretch of a year is not throwaway time. It's a chance to complete assignments, repair focus, restore discipline, and re-center on what matters most. The way you finish this year will set the tone for how you begin the next one.

Finishing strong doesn't mean doing everything perfectly. It means doing what God has placed in front of you with excellence, gratitude, and intentionality until the last day. Don't mentally check out—press in.

Momentum isn't something you lose — it's something you choose.

Reflection Questions

1. What unfinished assignment do I need to complete before the year ends?

2. What mindset do I need to finish this year with strength and gratitude?

Author Quote — Coach David Angeron

"Don't just end the year — finish it."

NOVEMBER 26 — LEGACY REQUIRES YOU TO LIVE WITH THE END IN MIND

Life feels long until it doesn't. Numbering your days doesn't mean living in fear of death—it means living with clarity about life. When you remember that your time on earth is limited, your priorities become sharper. Petty distractions lose power. Eternal things gain weight.

Legacy leaders think about the day they will stand before God and give an account for their lives. That awareness changes how they steward time, relationships, resources, and assignments. They ask, "If my story ended soon, what would it say right now?"

Living with the end in mind doesn't rob you of joy—it protects it. It frees you from wasting years on what won't matter and pushes you to invest deeply in what will.

Living with the end in mind creates clarity today.

Reflection Questions

1. If my life ended today, what would my legacy currently reflect?

2. What change today would most impact my legacy tomorrow?

Author Quote — Coach David Angeron

"Legacy is created when you live today with eternity in mind."

November 27 — Legacy Is Built by Intentional Habits, Not Inspirational Moments

Inspiration is a great spark, but it's a terrible strategy. You can't build a lasting legacy on occasional bursts of passion. You build it on repeated, intentional habits that align with your calling.

Your daily decisions—how you spend your time, what you consume, how you treat people, how you seek God—are quietly shaping your future. You may not see the impact of one day, but you will see the impact of 365 days of faithfulness.

God often tests you in the "little" places before trusting you with the "much." When you steward small responsibilities with excellence, bigger ones begin to appear. Legacy is not about doing something big once—it's about doing the right things over and over again.

What you do daily is more powerful than what you do dramatically.

Reflection Questions

1. What daily habit is shaping the future I want?
2. What habit is holding my future back?

Author Quote — Coach David Angeron

"Legacy is written one habit at a time."

November 28 — Generosity Strengthens Legacy

"It is more blessed to give than to receive." — Acts 20:35

You can't build a powerful legacy with a closed hand. Generosity is one of the loudest echoes a life can leave behind. People may forget your titles, but they will not forget how you gave—your time, resources, encouragement, wisdom, opportunities, and compassion.

Generosity is not about how much you have; it's about how willing you are. Some of the greatest kingdom impact has come from people who didn't have abundance, but they had obedience. They shared, sowed, and served anyway.

When you live generously, you look like your Father. God so loved the world that He gave. Every time you give, you push back against selfishness and scarcity and step into kingdom thinking.

You don't need wealth to build legacy — you need willingness.

Reflection Questions

1. What can I give today that will impact someone's life tomorrow?
2. Where have I held back generosity out of fear or scarcity?

Author Quote — Coach David Angeron

"Legacy grows everywhere generosity flows."

November 29 — Legacy Leaders Think Beyond Themselves

"Look not only to your own interests, but also to the interests of others."
— Philippians 2:4

A small life is one that thinks only in terms of "me": my goals, my comfort, my success, my image. A legacy life thinks in terms of "we" and "they": How will this decision affect my family, my team, my community, the next generation?

Legacy leaders live outward-focused. They design systems that bless others, build organizations that serve people, and make decisions that consider who is coming behind them. Their vision is not just, "How will this benefit me now?" but "How will this benefit others later?"

Thinking beyond yourself doesn't mean neglecting your own needs—it means understanding that your life carries responsibility beyond your own story. The more God enlarges your influence, the more people your obedience will affect.

The greatest lives are lived for more than the person living them.

Reflection Questions

1. Who will benefit from the work I'm doing today — even years from now?

2. How can I shift from self-impact to multi-generational impact?

Author Quote — Coach David Angeron

"Legacy is leadership that outlives the leader."

November 30 — Legacy Is Measured by Faithfulness, Not Fame

"Well done, good and faithful servant." — Matthew 25:23

Heaven's words over your life won't be, "Well done, successful influencer," or "Well done, widely known leader." The words we're all longing to hear are simple and powerful: "Well done, good and faithful servant."

Faithfulness is showing up when no one sees. It's doing what God asked you to do even when it doesn't trend, doesn't impress, and doesn't give you instant rewards. Some of the greatest legacy builders in the kingdom will never be widely recognized on earth—but heaven knows their names.

Fame is a poor measurement of impact. God doesn't weigh your follower count; He weighs your obedience. Did you love well? Did you serve faithfully? Did you steward what He gave you? Did you say yes when it cost you?

Impact is not measured by audience size — but by obedience level.

Reflection Questions

1. Am I chasing influence or practicing faithfulness?
2. What has God asked me to do that requires steady obedience?

Author Quote — Coach David Angeron

"God doesn't reward fame — He rewards faithfulness."

DECEMBER

REFLECTION, RENEWAL & VISION FOR THE NEW YEAR

December 1 — Gratitude Positions the Heart for Breakthrough

"In everything give thanks." — 1 Thessalonians 5:18

Gratitude is not denial of reality — it is a decision about focus. When you give thanks "in everything," you are not thanking God *for* every circumstance, but choosing to see Him *in* every circumstance. Gratitude shifts your perspective from what's missing to what God is moving. It pulls your attention away from lack and places it on evidence of His faithfulness.

You cannot stay thankful and stay stuck in self-pity at the same time. Gratitude loosens the grip of discouragement, entitlement, and comparison. It opens the heart to expect God to move again. A grateful heart is a soft heart — and a soft heart can receive new direction, new strength, and new joy.

Gratitude is worship in motion. It is your way of saying, "God, I see Your hand — and I trust Your heart."

Reflection Questions

1. What blessing have I overlooked lately?

2. What has God done this year that I need to thank Him for again?

Author Quote — Coach David Angeron

"Gratitude doesn't change your situation — it changes your spirit in the situation."

December 2 — Celebrate Progress, Not Just Perfection

God is not waiting for you to become flawless before He delights in you. He rejoices over steps, not just finishes. Heaven celebrates when you choose obedience instead of old patterns, when you show up one more day, when you repent, when you grow—even if you're still in process.

Perfectionism blinds you to progress. It convinces you that "it's not enough," so you never celebrate how far God has already brought you. But progress is proof of God's work in your life. When you learn to honor small wins—one habit corrected, one boundary set, one apology made—you build momentum instead of discouragement.

Celebrating progress doesn't mean you lower the standard; it means you acknowledge the journey. The more you recognize God's work step by step, the more encouraged you are to keep moving.

When you celebrate progress, motivation accelerates.

Reflection Questions

1. What progress this year have I not acknowledged or celebrated?

2. What small win can I intentionally honor today?

Author Quote — Coach David Angeron

"Progress is worthy of celebration, even before perfection arrives."

December 3 — Don't Let This Year End Without Praise

The year may not have gone exactly how you planned—but God has been present in every chapter. Before you rush into new goals, visions, and requests, pause and praise. Praise forces your soul to remember what your emotions often forget: God has been faithful.

Think about the prayers God answered, the doors He opened, the dangers you avoided, the peace He provided, the strength you didn't have on your own. Some miracles were obvious. Others were hidden in protection, redirection, or the grace simply to endure. None of it was random.

When you end a year in praise, you refuse to let disappointment write the final word. Praise reframes your memory: you don't just see the battles—you see the God who carried you through them.

Gratitude today fuels confidence for tomorrow.

Reflection Questions

1. What prayers did God answer this year that I haven't fully praised Him for?

2. What miracle or moment deserves renewed thanksgiving?

Author Quote — Coach David Angeron

"Praise is how you end a year in victory — no matter what happened."

DECEMBER 4 — WORSHIP BRINGS CLARITY WHEN LIFE BRINGS QUESTIONS

"God is enthroned on the praises of His people." — Psalm 22:3

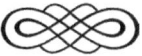

Questions, confusion, and uncertainty are part of every leader's journey. But clarity doesn't begin with more analysis; it begins with more adoration. When you worship, you are not ignoring the problem—you are elevating God above it. You are reminding your soul, "He is still in control."

In worship, your focus shifts from "What will I do?" to "Who is with me?" Doubt loses its volume when God's character fills the room. Fear loosens its grip when you magnify the One who never changes. Often, God will give direction *after* worship because your heart is finally still enough to hear.

Worship doesn't change who God is—it changes how you see Him. And when your view of God gets bigger, your confusion gets smaller.

Clarity often comes through worship before it comes through answers.

Reflection Questions

1. Do I worship only when I feel it, or because God deserves it?

2. In what area of my life do I need clarity that worship can unlock?

Author Quote — Coach David Angeron

"Worship doesn't remind God who He is — it reminds us who He is."

December 5 — What You Thank God For, God Multiplies

"And He gave thanks… and it multiplied." — Matthew 14:19

Before the miracle of feeding thousands, Jesus didn't complain about what He lacked—He thanked the Father for what He had. Gratitude turned "not enough" into "more than enough." That's a kingdom pattern. Complaining shrinks your perspective; thanksgiving expands your expectation.

When you treat God's blessings as ordinary or insufficient, your heart closes to increase. But when you genuinely thank Him for what's in your hands—relationships, opportunities, resources, even "small" wins—you're recognizing Him as the Source. And God loves to pour more into the hands of a grateful steward.

This doesn't mean we manipulate God with gratitude. It means we align our hearts with His goodness and create room to receive. You start seeing how much He's already done—and faith rises for what He can still do.

Thankfulness is the doorway to more.

Reflection Questions

1. What blessing have I treated as ordinary instead of multiplying through gratitude?

2. What can I thank God for today that I've taken for granted?

Author Quote — Coach David Angeron

"Whatever you complain about shrinks — whatever you thank God for grows."

DECEMBER 6 —
REFLECTION IS A FORM OF WORSHIP

"I will remember the deeds of the Lord." — Psalm 77:11

Life moves fast, and in survival mode, you rarely stop to see how much God has already done. Reflection slows you down long enough to trace God's fingerprints across your year. Every closed door that protected you, every unexpected opportunity that lifted you, every moment of strength that didn't come from you—these are all reasons to worship.

Remembering is holy work. When you reflect, you turn memory into praise. You start to see that you were never alone—that even on the days you felt abandoned, God was carrying you. Reflection also builds confidence: if He was faithful then, He will be faithful again.

Looking back isn't about living in the past; it's about recognizing grace in the past so you can walk with faith into the future.

Look back just long enough to see God's fingerprints.

Reflection Questions

1. What moment this year proved that God was with me?

2. How has God grown or matured me over the last 12 months?

Author Quote — Coach David Angeron

"Reflection reveals God's faithfulness that you missed while surviving."

DECEMBER 7 — GOD DESERVES PRAISE BEFORE YOU RECEIVE THE PROMISE

"Let everything that has breath praise the Lord." — Psalm 150:6

Anyone can praise God after the promotion, the healing, the breakthrough, or the answered prayer. Faith praises *before* it sees the results. When you praise God in advance, you are saying, "I trust Your character more than I trust my circumstances."

Praising in the middle of uncertainty confuses the enemy. He expects you to complain, doubt, and retreat—yet you worship. That worship declares that God is worthy regardless of timelines, outcomes, or feelings. It shifts your posture from desperation to expectation.

Praise is not a reward you give God for doing what you hoped. It's the response you give because of who He already is. And often, that atmosphere of faith is where doors start to open and hearts begin to shift.

Praising in advance prepares the atmosphere for breakthrough.

Reflection Questions

1. What have I been waiting to praise God for until I see results?
2. How can I worship even while waiting?

Author Quote — Coach David Angeron

"Don't wait for the victory to praise — praise is part of the victory."

DECEMBER 8 — JOY IS A WEAPON

"The joy of the Lord is your strength." — Nehemiah 8:10

Joy is not shallow happiness based on good days and easy circumstances. Joy is a deep, inner confidence that God is present, faithful, and in control—even when life feels unstable. That kind of joy becomes a weapon in spiritual battles.

The enemy wants you exhausted, discouraged, and joyless because a joyless believer is an easy target. But when you fight to protect joy—through worship, gratitude, Scripture, and community—you fight to protect your strength. Joy is how your heart says, "God is still good, and I'm still standing."

You don't have to pretend everything feels great to walk in joy. You simply have to anchor your heart in the reality of who God is. When joy rises, fear, despair, and defeat begin to lose their grip.

Joy doesn't mean life is perfect — it means God is present.

Reflection Questions

1. What has been stealing my joy recently?

2. What practice consistently restores joy in my life?

Author Quote — Coach David Angeron

"Joy isn't a feeling — it's fuel."

DECEMBER 9 —
GRATITUDE KILLS ANXIETY

"With thanksgiving… the peace of God will guard your hearts and minds."
— Philippians 4:6–7

Anxiety thrives in a mind that constantly rehearses worst-case scenarios. Gratitude thrives in a mind that constantly rehearses God's goodness. Scripture doesn't just tell us to pray—it tells us to pray *with thanksgiving*. Why? Because thanksgiving shifts the atmosphere inside your mind.

When you start listing what God has done, how He's come through, what He's already provided, and how many times He's sustained you, worry begins to lose credibility. Fear cannot dominate a heart that is actively remembering God's track record.

Gratitude doesn't mean you ignore real concerns. It means you bring them to God while also acknowledging, "You have been faithful before, and I trust You now." That posture opens the floodgates for peace that doesn't even make sense based on circumstances.

When gratitude increases, anxiety decreases.

Reflection Questions

1. What blessing do I need to rehearse rather than replaying worry?

2. What anxiety can I surrender to God with thanksgiving today?

Author Quote — Coach David Angeron

"A grateful mind cannot be a fearful mind."

December 10 — Celebrate What God Did — Even If It Was Different Than You Expected

"My ways are higher than your ways." — Isaiah 55:9

We often assume God's answer will look like our idea. When it doesn't, we can miss the miracle because it's dressed in a different form. Maybe the relationship didn't work, but God protected you. Maybe the door closed, but it redirected you to something better. Maybe the timing changed, but it preserved you from burnout or disaster.

Faith doesn't just celebrate when God does what you pictured. Faith celebrates when you recognize His wisdom, even when the path surprised you. Looking back over the year, there are situations you wanted to go one way—but in hindsight, God's way was safer, wiser, or more fruitful.

Maturity is learning to praise Him not only for what He did, but for what He didn't allow.

Just because it didn't happen your way doesn't mean God didn't move.

Reflection Questions

1. What did God do this year that I didn't appreciate because it didn't look like I expected?

2. What unexpected blessing came from a disappointment?

Author Quote — Coach David Angeron

"God's plan worked — even when it didn't look like mine."

December 11 — Worship Turns Waiting Into Trust

"Those who hope in the Lord will renew their strength." — Isaiah 40:31

Waiting can feel like a waste—unless you understand what God is doing in it. The waiting room is where God grows your trust, refines your motives, and strengthens your dependency on Him. But how you wait matters.

If you spend your waiting season complaining, comparing, and doubting, the delay will drain you. If you spend it worshiping, the same delay will develop you. Worship in waiting says, "God, even if I don't see movement yet, I believe You are working."

Worship takes your eyes off the clock and puts them back on Christ. Your heart shifts from, "When will this happen?" to "Who am I becoming while I wait?" When you hope in the Lord, your strength is renewed—not by an answer but by His presence.

Trust grows in the waiting room.

Reflection Questions

1. Where has waiting weakened my trust instead of strengthening it?

2. How can I use worship to turn waiting into growth?

Author Quote — Coach David Angeron

"Waiting is not wasted when you worship while you wait."

December 12 —
Make Space for God's Presence

"Draw near to God, and He will draw near to you." — James 4:8

G od is not distant, disinterested, or hard to reach. He promises that when you draw near to Him, He responds. But closeness with God doesn't happen accidentally—it happens intentionally. Your schedule will not auto-create space for His presence; you must carve it out.

Just like your body weakens without food and water, your spirit weakens without time in God's presence. Prayer, worship, Scripture, silence, and listening are not religious boxes to check—they are lifelines. His presence brings wisdom for decisions, comfort for pain, correction for drift, and strength for calling.

Ask yourself honestly: is God getting the margins of your time or the priority of your time? When you treat His presence as essential, everything else in your life begins to align.

Your soul needs the presence of God more than your body needs oxygen.

Reflection Questions

1. What competes most for my time with God?

2. What simple rhythm can I add to create more space for Him?

Author Quote — Coach David Angeron

"God's presence isn't found in the margins — it's found in the moments you make."

DECEMBER 13 — FINISH THE YEAR WITH WORSHIP, NOT WORRY

"Cast all your anxiety on Him because He cares for you." — 1 Peter 5:7

You don't have to drag this year's stress into next year's story. The burdens, regrets, disappointments, and unresolved fears you're still carrying weren't designed to cross every finish line with you. God invites you to cast—throw, release, hand over—every anxiety to Him.

Worry keeps rehearsing what went wrong. Worship releases it into God's hands. When you choose worship at the end of a year, you're choosing to close the chapter with trust instead of tension. You're saying, "God, I didn't understand everything that happened, but I trust Your care more than my questions."

Finishing in worship doesn't change the past—but it transforms your posture for the future. It clears space in your heart for new assignments, fresh faith, and deeper peace.

What you release now determines what you can receive next.

Reflection Questions

1. What burden have I been holding that God is asking me to release?

2. What would shift in my life if I finished the year in worship instead of worry?

Author Quote — Coach David Angeron

"The year doesn't end in defeat — it ends in worship."

December 14 — Celebration Is Spiritual Warfare

"Rejoice in the Lord always." — Philippians 4:4

Rejoicing is more than a mood—it's a weapon. When you choose to celebrate God's goodness, you are pushing back against heaviness, despair, and spiritual attack. Celebration says, "Devil, you tried—but God still wins."

You don't rejoice because everything went perfectly. You rejoice because, despite everything that happened, God never left, never failed, and never lost control. That act of joy is not naivety; it's warfare. It declares that your hope is not tied to circumstances but anchored in Christ.

Think back over this year: the victories, the answered prayers, the lessons learned, the strength you gained. Celebrate those moments on purpose. The more you celebrate God's faithfulness, the more your faith rises for the future.

Your praise is a problem for the enemy.

Reflection Questions

1. What victory this year deserves to be celebrated again?

2. How can I celebrate God intentionally this week?

Author Quote — Coach David Angeron

"Celebration is proof that the enemy didn't win."

December 15 — Worship Prepares You for What's Next

How you close one season affects how you enter the next. Worship is the doorway between chapters. Thanksgiving and praise are how you step into God's presence, reset your heart, and align your spirit for what's ahead.

When you end the year in frustration, exhaustion, or bitterness, you carry that weight into the next one. But when you end it in worship, you step over the threshold with renewed faith. Looking back in gratitude reminds you that God has been faithful. Looking forward in praise reminds you that He will continue to be.

Worship clears out clutter—fear, disappointment, control—and makes room for fresh vision. It prepares your mind, emotions, and spirit to receive new assignments, new strategies, and new levels of trust.

How you end this year determines how you begin the next.

Reflection Questions

1. What blessing from this year should shape my faith for next year?

2. What mindset shift do I need to carry into the new season?

Author Quote — Coach David Angeron

"Worship closes one chapter and opens the next with victory."

December 16 — Gratitude Turns the Page on Every Painful Chapter

"You have turned my mourning into dancing." — Psalm 30:11

You cannot rewrite what happened this year, but you *can* rewrite how it sits in your heart. Gratitude doesn't erase grief, betrayal, loss, or disappointment—but it refuses to let those moments become the headline of your story. When you look back through the lens of gratitude, you start to see details you missed in the middle of the pain: the people who showed up, the strength you didn't know you had, the peace that carried you, the doors God closed to protect you, the tears that watered new wisdom.

Gratitude doesn't say, "That pain was good." It says, "God was good *even there.*" It transforms events from "That broke me" into "That built me." Your painful chapters are not the end of your story; they become the places where God's faithfulness shines brightest.

Gratitude transforms pain into testimony.

Reflection Questions

1. What painful moment from this year actually revealed God's goodness?

2. How did God carry me through what I thought would break me?

Author Quote — Coach David Angeron

"Gratitude doesn't deny pain — it declares that pain didn't win."

December 17 — Don't Forget the Prayers You Prayed That God Answered

"Bless the Lord... forget not all His benefits." — Psalm 103:2

At the start of this year, there were things you were desperately asking God for—open doors, provision, clarity, strength, healing, opportunities, relationships, help. Some of those things you are standing in right now. What used to be a prayer is now normal. What used to be an emergency is now a testimony.

But if you're not careful, you'll move so quickly to the "next" request that you never pause to honor the "now" answer. Forgetfulness starves gratitude. Remembering fuels worship. Take time to rewind: the bills that got paid, the moments you almost quit but didn't, the times God protected you from what you wanted, the peace that showed up when it shouldn't have.

You are walking through answered prayers that once kept you up at night. Don't rush past them. Name them. Thank God for them. Share them.

Your testimony deserves to be remembered.

Reflection Questions

1. What answered prayer am I living in right now?

2. Who needs to hear the testimony of what God did?

Author Quote — Coach David Angeron

"Yesterday's miracles deserve today's praise."

December 18 — Don't Let the Enemy Steal What God Restored

This year, God may have restored parts of your life that were once broken—your peace, your identity, your confidence, your sense of calling, your relationships, your joy. Restoration is not just a moment; it's a new foundation. But what God restores, the enemy will always try to erode—through distraction, temptation, old patterns, and subtle compromises.

The enemy doesn't always need to destroy you outright; sometimes he just needs you to drift until you slowly surrender what God gave back. That's why you must guard your restoration with boundaries, spiritual disciplines, and wise relationships. Protect your mind. Protect your habits. Protect your time with God.

What God healed, don't reopen. What God freed you from, don't entertain. Reinforce what God restored with obedience and focus.

Guard your restoration.

Reflection Questions

1. What has God restored in my life that needs protecting?
2. What distraction or temptation threatens that restoration?

Author Quote — Coach David Angeron

"What God restores, you must reinforce."

December 19 — Celebrate What God Did Privately, Not Just Publicly

"Your Father, who sees what is done in secret, will reward you." — Matthew 6:6

Some of the most important victories this year didn't happen on a platform, in a meeting, or on social media. They happened in quiet spaces—when you forgave someone no one else knew about, when you chose purity over compromise, when you said no to an old temptation, when you kept going on a day you wanted to quit, when you prayed through tears instead of numbing the pain.

Those secret moments are sacred. Heaven saw every choice, every battle, every small yes that no one clapped for. God is not impressed by public image; He is moved by private obedience. The world may never know how hard some days were, but God does—and He calls those hidden victories powerful.

Take time to celebrate the work God did *inside* you, not just *around* you. Quiet growth is still supernatural growth.

Private battles won are just as worthy of praise as public victories.

Reflection Questions

1. What quiet victory from this year deserves to be honored?

2. What healing or growth took place that wasn't visible to others?

Author Quote — Coach David Angeron

"The victories no one sees are often the most powerful ones."

December 20 — God Was Working Even When You Didn't Feel It

"We walk by faith, not by sight." — 2 Corinthians 5:7

There were days this year when your emotions said, "God is distant. God is silent. God is not moving." But your feelings are not the final authority—God's faithfulness is. Often, His most strategic work is done under the surface: shifting relationships, closing wrong doors, healing wounds, testing motives, strengthening character, setting up opportunities that haven't appeared yet.

You may not have felt goosebumps, but you gained grit. You may not have heard a loud word, but you learned to trust in the quiet. Looking back, there are moments that felt like chaos then but look like divine alignment now. That's proof that God was working even when your emotions disagreed.

Faith doesn't walk by what it feels or sees in the moment; it walks by who God has already proven Himself to be.

Silence wasn't abandonment — it was strategy.

Reflection Questions

1. When did my feelings lie to me about what God was doing?

2. What can I now see clearly that I couldn't see in the moment?

Author Quote — Coach David Angeron

"God's silence is not God's absence — it is His strategy."

December 21 — God Did More This Year Than You Realize

"Surely goodness and mercy shall follow me." — Psalm 23:6

Y ou are aware of a few big victories from this year—but heaven's highlight reel is much longer. God's goodness has been trailing you in ways you never noticed: the accident that didn't happen, the deal that fell through that would have trapped you, the relationship that ended before it could derail you, the spiritual attacks that never reached you.

We often only praise God for the visible miracles, forgetting that His mercy was quietly working all year long. Goodness followed you into rooms you didn't deserve to be in. Mercy covered mistakes that could have disqualified you. Protection surrounded situations you thought were random.

Ask God to open your eyes to the "invisible" blessings—the near misses, the subtle shifts, the closed doors that were actually shields. The more you look, the more you'll realize: He did far more than you knew.

A lot went right this year that you didn't even know about.

Reflection Questions

1. What blessing or protection did I only recognize later?

2. In what area of life can I spot God's fingerprints now?

Author Quote — Coach David Angeron

"The proof of God's goodness is often seen looking backward."

December 22 — A Grateful Heart Finishes Strong

"Give thanks to the Lord, for He is good." — Psalm 136:1

Finishing strong is not just about energy—it's about attitude. A resentful heart drags into the finish line, replaying what went wrong. A grateful heart crosses the line declaring, "God was good to me, even here." You may not have had a perfect year, but you *do* have a faithful God.

Gratitude strengthens your endurance. It keeps you from quitting in disappointment or sitting in self-pity. It trains your mind to notice God's goodness more than the enemy's attacks. It allows you to close this year with worship instead of cynicism, with hope instead of heaviness.

You don't finish strong because everything went right; you finish strong because you refuse to let what went wrong define you. A grateful heart sees this year not as wasted, but as woven into God's bigger story.

End the year with worship, not weariness.

Reflection Questions

1. Is my heart finishing the year grateful or resentful?

2. What gratitude declaration will I carry into the new year?

Author Quote — Coach David Angeron

"A grateful heart always outlasts a difficult year."

December 23 —
Worship Is the Sound of Victory
Before the Battle Ends

"The shout of the King is among them!" — Numbers 23:21

In Scripture, God's people often shouted *before* the breakthrough—before Jericho's walls fell, before the sea opened, before enemies were defeated. Worship wasn't just a celebration of victory; it was the sound that preceded it. Heaven responds to faith-filled praise.

When you worship in the middle of the battle, you're declaring, "God's promise is more real to me than my problem." You refuse to let fear or fatigue set the tone. Instead, you let the shout of the King—the presence and authority of Jesus—define the atmosphere.

Worship in warfare is not about volume; it's about agreement. You are agreeing with what God said instead of what circumstances say. That kind of worship doesn't just comfort you—it pushes back darkness and invites heaven's intervention.

Worship is spiritual confidence.

Reflection Questions

1. Where do I need to worship God before the breakthrough arrives?

2. How would my prayer life change if I worshiped from victory instead of for victory?

Author Quote — Coach David Angeron

"Victory has a sound — and that sound is worship."

December 24 — Make Room for Jesus Before the New Year Begins

"Seek first the kingdom of God." — Matthew 6:33

The end of the year is often crowded—events, deadlines, travel, busyness. It's easy to squeeze Jesus into leftover moments and call it devotion. But kingdom order is clear: *seek first*. Before you sketch goals, vision boards, or strategies for next year, ask a deeper question: "Where is Jesus in my priorities?"

Making room for Him doesn't just mean a one-time decision; it means rearranging your schedule, your habits, and even some relationships to put Him at the center. When Jesus is first, everything else finds its place. Peace flows more freely. Decisions gain clarity. Temptations lose some of their power.

Don't wait for a calendar reset to reset your heart. End this year walking closely with Him, so you enter the next already aligned.

The greatest preparation for a new season is presence, not planning.

Reflection Questions

1. What needs to decrease so Jesus can increase in my life?

2. What spiritual rhythm will I begin now instead of "next year"?

Author Quote — Coach David Angeron

"The best way to enter a new year is already walking with Jesus."

DECEMBER 25 — JESUS IS THE GREATEST GIFT YOU WILL EVER RECEIVE

"For unto us a child is born… and He will be called Wonderful Counselor, Mighty God, Everlasting Father, Prince of Peace." — Isaiah 9:6

Christmas is more than a tradition, a story, or a sentimental moment—it is the celebration of God stepping into human history to rescue us. Jesus didn't come just to inspire you; He came to save you, transform you, and walk with you. Every title in Isaiah 9:6 reveals a need He came to meet: wisdom for confusion, power for weakness, a Father's love for loneliness, peace for inner chaos.

Presents under a tree eventually fade, break, or get forgotten. But the presence of Christ in your life is eternal. He is the gift who forgives sins, heals hearts, restores purpose, and anchors your identity.

This Christmas, don't just acknowledge Jesus—embrace Him. Invite Him into your decisions, your pain, your dreams, and your future.

Christmas is not an event — it's the reminder that God came close.

Reflection Questions

1. What does Jesus mean to me personally — beyond tradition?
2. How can I honor Him in my life beyond the holiday season?

Author Quote — Coach David Angeron

"Jesus is not a gift under the tree — He is the gift who hung on a tree."

December 26 — You Didn't Just Survive This Year — You Grew

"The righteous will flourish like a palm tree." — Psalm 92:12

It's easy to look back and think, "I barely made it." But survival isn't the full story. In every challenge, God was stretching your capacity. In every delay, He was strengthening your patience. In every trial, He was deepening your roots. Palm trees bend in storms but don't break — and that's what happened in you.

You grew in ways you didn't notice: you respond differently now, you discern faster, you recover quicker, you pray deeper, you trust sooner. That's growth. Flourishing doesn't always look like fireworks; sometimes it looks like quiet resilience.

Don't downplay the work God has done in you just because it doesn't feel dramatic. You are not who you were twelve months ago—and that's evidence of His hand on your life.

God didn't just get you through this year — He grew you through this year.

Reflection Questions

1. What quality in me is noticeably stronger today than it was a year ago?

2. What did this year teach me that I want to carry into the future?

Author Quote — Coach David Angeron

"Every season strengthened you — even the ones that stretched you."

December 27 — Don't Drag Old Chains Into a New Year

"He who the Son sets free is free indeed." — John 8:36

Freedom is costly—Jesus paid for it with His life. Don't dishonor that freedom by choosing to live in chains He already broke. Regret, shame, old mentalities, toxic cycles, and unhealthy relationships do not deserve a ticket into the next season. If you carry them forward, they will choke what God is trying to grow.

New seasons call for new mindsets. That doesn't mean you forget everything—it means you refuse to be *defined* by it. You apply the lessons, receive the forgiveness, walk in the healing, and release what no longer aligns with where God is taking you.

Before you step into a new year, do a spiritual inventory: "What has God already freed me from that I keep revisiting?" Then, by His grace, let it go.

New wine requires new wineskins.

Reflection Questions

1. What do I need to leave behind before I step into the next year?

2. What freedom did God give me this year that I refuse to surrender again?

Author Quote — Coach David Angeron

"If God broke the chain, don't keep holding it."

December 28 — Tomorrow Belongs to the Faithful

The future doesn't ultimately belong to the talented, the connected, or the lucky—it belongs to the faithful. God establishes the steps of those who commit their plans, their work, and their schedules to Him. That commitment is not a casual prayer; it's a daily surrender of, "Lord, this belongs to You first."

Faithfulness looks like showing up when it's not glamorous, obeying when it's not easy, and honoring God when no one else sees. When you live that way, your tomorrow is not random—it's guided. You may not know all the details of next year, but you *do* know the One directing it.

As you look ahead, don't just dream—*dedicate*. Place your plans in God's hands and ask Him to align, prune, and bless what reflects His will.

The future is bright when the foundation is Christ.

Reflection Questions

1. What am I committing to the Lord for next year?
2. What discipline or habit will position me for the future God is building?

Author Quote — Coach David Angeron

"The future is not for the lucky — it is for the faithful."

December 29 — Step Into the New Year Boldly

"Be strong and courageous… for the Lord your God is with you wherever you go."
— Joshua 1:9

You are not stepping into an unknown future alone—you are stepping with the God who has never left your side. Fear will try to follow you into the new year, whispering, "What if you fail? What if it falls apart? What if you're not enough?" But courage doesn't come from guarantees; it comes from God's presence.

Boldness is not recklessness. It's obedient confidence. It's deciding, "Because God is with me, I will not tiptoe into what He has prepared. I will move with faith." That may mean launching the thing, having the conversation, applying for the opportunity, writing the book, starting the ministry, or making the change.

Don't let last year's fears dictate next year's steps. Step in like someone who knows their Father goes before them.

The door ahead is not empty — it is prepared.

Reflection Questions

1. What fear do I refuse to carry into the new year?
2. What bold step of faith will I take in the first 30 days of the new year?

Author Quote — Coach David Angeron

"Don't tiptoe into the future — run toward what God has prepared."

December 30 — This Is Not the End — It's the Launchpad

"He who began a good work in you will carry it on to completion."
— Philippians 1:6

The end of the year can feel final, like a finish line. But in the kingdom, every ending is really a launching point. God didn't just *begin* a good work in you this year—He intends to *continue* it. What He developed in you—discipline, humility, resilience, wisdom, hunger for His presence—are not random traits. They are equipment for the next assignment.

You are not closing a story; you are turning a page. This year prepared you in ways you may not fully see yet. The lessons you learned, the battles you fought, the character you built—God plans to use all of it.

So instead of saying, "I'm done," say, "I'm ready." Ready for deeper impact, clearer purpose, more courage, and greater obedience.

Your best chapter isn't behind you — it's ahead of you.

Reflection Questions

1. What am I believing God for in the upcoming year?

2. In one sentence, who am I committing to become next year?

Author Quote — Coach David Angeron

"This year developed you — next year will deploy you."

DECEMBER 31 — THE FINAL AMEN

The end of the year isn't just a closing chapter — it's a celebration of God's faithfulness and a declaration of what's to come. Looking back reminds you of what God brought you through. Looking forward reminds you of what God is leading you into.

You are here because grace carried you.

You are stronger because trials refined you.

You are wiser because lessons shaped you.

You are equipped because God prepared you.

This year had victories and valleys — yet God never left you for a moment. Not once. He was with you on the mountaintop and in the midnight. He sustained you, protected you, guided you, corrected you, lifted you, and positioned you.

And the same God who walked with you this year will walk with you into the next. Tonight is not about fear of the unknown — it is about faith in the God who already knows. The future is not uncertain when the path is lit by the presence of God.

End this year with praise — begin the next with purpose.

Reflection Questions

1. What final praise do I want to offer God for this year?

2. What word, focus, or declaration will define the next year of my life?

Author Quote — Coach David Angeron

"If God was faithful this year, He will be faithful next year — and every year after."

Conclusion —
Built to Lead Differently

Leadership is not proven by titles, achievements, revenue, or reputation.

Leadership is proven by **character, consistency, and calling.**

Over the last 365 days, you have prayed bold prayers… asked courageous questions… and confronted the parts of leadership that most people avoid. You have chosen the difficult growth over the easy path, discipline over comfort, faith over fear, and excellence over approval. You have led from the spirit — not just the skill.

And that's what makes you **Built Different.**

You are not a leader by accident.

You are not gifted by coincidence.

You are not called without purpose.

God has planted you in the marketplace for influence, impact, and eternal purpose. Your business is more than business — it is ministry disguised as leadership. Every decision, every opportunity, every relationship, and every responsibility is a chance to reflect Christ in the workplace and advance the Kingdom through excellence.

You are here to:
- Build people.
- Build culture.
- Build legacy.
- Build companies that honor God.

And you will — because God built *you* for this.

The world does not need more bosses.

The world does not need more celebrities.

The world does not need more titles.

The world needs **leaders with backbone, compassion, emotional strength, spiritual maturity, and unwavering faith.**

Leaders who pray before they plan.

Leaders who serve before they speak.

Leaders who hold the line when others break.

Leaders who choose obedience when others choose popularity.

That's who you are becoming — day by day, decision by decision, prayer by prayer.

And the best part?

God is not done with you.

If this year has proven anything, it's this:

- **You are capable of more than you thought.**
- **God is closer than you realized.**
- **Your leadership is bigger than your position.**

The next chapter of your life will demand even more faith, vision, courage, and discipline — and you are ready for it.

Not because of talent.

Not because of strategy.

Not because of ambition.

But because **God built you different.**

Walk boldly.

Lead courageously.

Influence intentionally.

Serve humbly.

Build faithfully.

And when you look back — on the businesses you built, the people you shaped, and the legacy you established — you will know without question:

It was God, through you, for His glory.

You are Built Different. Now go lead like it.

Final Closing Prayer

Father, thank You for Your goodness, Your mercy, Your guidance, and Your strength this year. I close this year with worship, and I enter the next year with faith. Order my steps, renew my mind, protect my purpose, and surround me with Your presence. I commit my life, my leadership, my family, my work, and my calling to You. Let Your will be done — in me and through me. In Jesus' name, Amen.

www.ingramcontent.com/pod-product-compliance
Lightning Source LLC
Chambersburg PA
CBHW060403130626
46555CB00005B/1982